EDUCATION

EVOLUTION, DEVELOPMENT & PHILOSOPHY

EDUCATION

Evolution, Development & Philosophy

Bhawna Misra

AKANSHA PUBLISHING HOUSE
NEW DELHI-110 059 (INDIA)

AKANSHA PUBLISHING HOUSE
R-37B, Vani Vihar, Uttam Nagar
New Delhi-110059
Phones: 56065579, 9811582579
Email: ektabooks@yahoo.com

Education: Evolution, Development and Philosophy

First Published 2004

ISBN 81-87606-46-0

PRINTED IN INDIA

Published by M.P. Misra for Akansha Publishing House, New Delhi-110059 and Printed at Tarun Offset Press, Delhi.

Contents

Preface

1. Education and Knowledge Explosion 1
2. The Intellectual and Moral Revolution in Education 18
3. Education during Ninth to Twelfth Centuries 82
4. Pride and Prejudice in Education 106
5. Education and Function of the School 123
6. Education at the Crossroads 138
7. Heredity and Education 164
8. Unity and Diversity in Modern Intellectual Discipline 177
9. Educational Aims and Cultural Postures 210

Bibliography 222

Index 224

Preface

The argument that learning is recollecting is itself tied up with some view about the sense's inadequacy to yield knowledge on certain topics, and about the objects of sense observation not properly exemplifying the properties of Forms. In other words, the argument about recollection seems to form a part Plato's polemic against sense-perception and the physical world, in contrast with the unchanging perfect-paradigm world of intellection.

Education is a very basic instinct imbedded in human nature/blood. How education emerged as an institution? It's with the history of human evolution and development. Development of civic sense of primitive man gradually transformed into institutionalized education system.

Here we have gathered choicest essays encompassing evolution, development of education.

Students, researchers, teachers will find this compilation of utmost use. We owe a deep sense of gratitude of all doyens, stalwarts who shaped the education and educational philosophy.

The publisher deserves all appreciation to bring out this book with all niceties.

—Editor

1

Education and Knowledge Explosion

"Knowledge is of two kinds. We know a subject ourselves, or we know where we can find information upon it."

—Samuel Johnson

The great social changes that have been reshaping the world today, one axis of change. . . which has great implications for all modern industrial societies, is the new impact of "knowledge"—its organization through systematic research guided by theory, and its mass dissemination through schools, publishing houses, and mass media. Where it concerns the educational system, the nature of this "knowledge revolution" can be explored from four angles: the "exponential growth" of knowledge, the "branching" of new fields of knowledge, the rise of a new intellectual technology, and the rapid expansion of research and development as an organized activity.

The "exponential growth" of knowledge is now a prosaic idea. Derek Price, who popularized it, has estimated (in *Science Since Babylon*) that the total research effort in Great Britain since the time of Newton has doubled every ten to fifteen years (or about three times during the working life of a scientist). A major indicator of this expansion has been the scientific journal. The learned paper and the scientific journal were innovations of the scientific revolution in the late seventeenth century. It allowed for the relatively rapid communication of new ideas to a growing circle of men interested in science. From the first few journals, beginning with the *Transactions of the Royal Society of London* in 1665, the number grew until by the beginning of the nineteenth century there were a hundred, by the middle of the nineteenth century a thousand, and by 1900 some ten thousand such journals.

Since 1750, when there were about ten scientific journals in the world, the number has increased by a factor of ten every half century. By 1830, when about three hundred journals were being published in the world, it became obvious that the cultivated man of science could no longer keep abreast of new knowledge, and a new device—the abstract journal—appeared. It summarized each article in many journals, and the interested individual could then decide what to read in full. But as Price points out, even the number of abstract journals increased, following the same logistic curve, by a factor of ten in every century. Thus by 1950 the number of abstract journals had attained a critical magnitude of about three hundred. Moreover, each abstract journal itself has sizably increased. A journal devoted to publishing the abstracts of new papers in the chemical sciences now runs to some 13,000 pages annually, exclusive of indexes and cross-references; ten years ago it was only half this size.

The output of sheer words today is staggering. In 1964, nearly 320,000 separate book titles—nearly 1,000 works every day—were published throughout the world. Columbia University's new acquisitions, for example, take up two miles of bookshelves a year. In a single field, medicine, it is estimated that some 200,000 journal articles and 10,000 monographs are published annually, while in the physical and life sciences the number of books add up to about 60,000 annually, the number of research reports to about 100,000 and the number of articles in scientific and technical journals to about 1.2 million each year. Consider what will happen when writers, scholars, scientists, and professionals in the new states begin to produce in great number in these fields!

But it is not the prodigious accumulation alone that is creating a distinctive change in the structure of intellectual life. It is the fact that new discoveries bring their own differentiation, or "branching," so that as a field expands subdivision and subspecialties multiply within each field. Contrary to the nineteenth-century notion of science as a bounded or exhaustible field of knowledge whose full dimensions can ultimately be explored, each advance opens up, in its own way, new fields that in turn sprout their own branches.

To give an example: the field of shock waves, initiated in 1848 by the British mathematician and physicist G.G. Stokes and the astronomer J. Challis (who set up theoretical equations of motion in gases), led not only to significant contributions in mathematics and physics along this general line (by Mach, Bethe, and von Neumann, among others) but to the branching off of shock tube, aerodynamics, detonations, and magnetohy- drodynamics as four distinct fields. Or, Nobel Laureate I.I. Rabi's success at Columbia, in 1929, in sending molecular beams through a magnetic field—a breakthrough in pure physics—gave rise to branching in several different directions: optics, solid state masers, atomic structures, and half a dozen other fields.

Sometimes a stasis is reached, and then a field spurts ahead. In 1895, Roentgen seemed to have exhausted all the major aspects of X-rays, but in 1912 the discovery of X-ray diffraction in crystals by Von Laue, Friedrich, and Knipping transformed two separate fields—X-ray and crystallography. Similarly, the discovery in 1934 of artificial radioactivity by the Joliot-Curies created a qualitative change that gave rise at one branching point to the work of Hahn and Strassman, which Lise Meitner correctly interpreted as the splitting of the uranium atom, and to Fermi's work on the increased radioactivity of metals bombarded with "slow" neutrons—which led directly to controlled atomic fission and the bomb.[1]

One can see this extraordinary proliferation of fields in the specializations listed in the National Register of Scientific and Technical Personnel, a government-sponsored inventory of all competent persons engaged in scientific work.[2] The Register classifies over 900 distinct scientific and technical specializations (outside the social sciences and humanities), compared with 54 listed twenty years ago. Thus physics is broken down into 10 basic divisions—acoustics, atomic and molecular, electromagnetic waves and electron, mechanics, nuclear, optics, physics of fluids, solid state, theoretical, and thermal phenomena—and each of these has subspecialities, making a total of 81 distinct specializations in physics alone. The life sciences are divided into 17 fields (e.g. anatomy, pharmacology, nutrition and metabolism, genetics, phytopathology) and each of these contains at least 10 or more subdivisions. In the newer interdisciplinary subjects, biophysics has 18 subspecialities, biochemistry 17, physical chemistry 26, geochemistry 7, oceanography 13, and hydrology and hydrography 12, while computer technology already has 7 subspecialities and the "mathematics of resource use" (operations research, information theory, and the like) has 13.

To the proliferation and branching of knowledge one can add the creation in recent years of what might be called a new "intellectual technology": the development of game theory, decision theory, simulation, linear programming, cybernetics, and operations research, many of which are tooled, as it were, by the computer. What makes the burgeoning of these fields significant is the effort, through novel intellectual techniques, to provide new and comprehensive theories of "rational choice" and to transform the social sciences in an unprecedented way.

Paradoxically, though this new intellectual revolution seeks "perfect" information, it starts out in vast linguistic disorder. Any eruptive change makes for great confusion, the more so in the new intellectual technology, since its innovators and practitioners are a motley pack of mathematicians, physicists, engineers (of all varieties), statisticians, biologists, neuro-physiologists, economists, management consultants, sociologists, and each man brings to the new field his own perspectives, terminology, and concepts.

Thus, operations research linear programming, systems analysis, and decision theory often overlap in technique and subject-matter, yet, depending upon the occupational origins of the practitioner, one or another label will be used insistently to designate a distinctive approach. Information theory, for some writers, is a technical set of propositions, enunciated originally by the electrical engineer Claude Shannon, on switching circuits and channel capacity; for others it is a general field covering all problems of interaction, and it is then called "communication theory." Cybernetics is regarded by some writers as the design of self-regulating control mechanisms (such as the automatic pilot on an airplane, which adjusts speed and direction in response to wind variation in order to stay on a plotted course); others call it the new "queen of science," embracing all self-regulating behavior from mechanical devices to biological organisms.

Whatever the final clarification of terminology will be, it is clear that the computer and these new techniques open up vast new possibilities for the social sciences. It is an equal corollary that all future work in the social sciences will require a high degree of mathematical training and sophistication. One area is the refinement of knowledge—the handling of many variables. Warren Weaver once said that an effective social science was almost impossible because as a mathematician he could handle a three-variable problem or, through statistical probability, a hundred variable problem, but that most of the interesting questions in the social sciences fell between three and a hundred. Thus, in charting voting behavior one could say that the relevant determinants are age, sex, religion, occupation, education and a dozen other variables; but it has been difficult to hold more than a few factors constant in order to see which combination of determinants was decisive in a voter's choice. With the computer, however, a matrix can be set up to handle a dozen or more variables.

One can go even further. With the computer, complex situations can be simulated, which might make possible "controlled" experiments in the social sciences. By "varying" the situations and introducing different "independent variables" one can see what new alignments and combinations of decisions might be made by groups in a simulated environment.

Simulation has been applied to a large variety of economic and sociological problems such as simulating an entire economy, charting demographic change, or predicting changes of attitudes in response to changed social environments. Professor Richard Stone, of Cambridge University, has created a simulation model of the British economy, and is thus in a position to state what changes in different sectors of the British economy are required to achieve different economic growth rates. A bold effort to simulate social environments through a computer program, and thus carry out a "controlled experiment" in the social sciences, has been made by James Coleman at Johns Hopkins. In his book *The Adolescent Society*, Coleman showed how students deliberately "choose" to stress popularity or scholastic achievement at the unspoken behest of the cliques they belong to, or by identifying with a teacher. To see how these students would alter their behavior, Coleman subsequently worked out a computer model in which the degree of identification of the adolescent with his clique (as expressed in the actual sociometric tests) was tested by varying the rewards from parents, teachers, or peer group influencing the adolescent. (Technically, Coleman established different "gambles" for the individual's "preference scales"). In this fashion he sought to specify, for example, at what exact points a student might be willing to sacrifice scholastic achievement for social popularity, and vice versa. While an experiment of this sort would normally be made with a small number of students, using only a few variables, Coleman was able, by creating "fictional" students (though using actual preference scales), to chart the different choices of thousands of "students" as they responded to a half dozen or so different variables, in numerous manipulated environments.

In the field of economics, various aspects of "decision theory" and "game theory" have already changed its dimensions. Linear programming, primarily an "ordering" technique to achieve optimal solutions where many alternative combinations confront a decision maker, is already widely used in business.[3] Statistical decision theory, as pioneered by the late Abraham Wald of Columbia University, sets forth strategies in "games against nature"—i.e., in situations partly subject to chance and only party controlled by the individual. With these techniques one can minimize risks and reduce uncertainty. And in the theory of games, initiated by the late John von Neumann, a revolution has begun in the definition of economics itself. An economic problem, as it is classically defined in general equilibrium theory, is one in which individuals and firms try to achieve "maximum" or optimal results. But the outcome of a man's actions depends not only on himself but on the actions of others as well. If two competitors follow a pure "maximizing" strategy it would lead, in the extreme, to a total victory or total defeat—the so-called zero-sum game. Von Newmann's theory of games, as Oskar Morgenstern has argued, signified a clear break in the development of economic thought, since under the conditions of competition or conflict the bent of "rational behavior" is to follow a so-called minimax strategy, which seeks to minimize losses, rather than the economic principle of seeking to maximize gains. "The structure of this theory," Morgenstern writes, "is, consequently, quite different from the current neo-classical one of general economic equilibrium. Lacking a new specify calculus, one has to fall back essentially on the fundamental, combinatorial elements of mathematical reasoning. Eventually, a new calculus may have to be invented or discovered, as specifically suited to economic-social problems as the differential calculus was to classical mechanics."[4]

If decision theory attempts to specify the best choices for a given premise, systems theory seeks to spell out the unified consequences of any choice for all the units in the system. The word "system" by now has the widest and most varied use of all the terms in the new intellectual vocabulary. It is used by engineers to denote complex devices like computing machines. ("Systems engineer" initially meant someone who can design or work on computers). Military technologists talk about weapons systems, sociologists about kinship or social systems, and economists, of course, about the economic system. But despite this great diversity, the foundation for a common conceptual framework in what Norbert Wiener has called "organized complexity" does exist.

Now, the idea of a system is an obvious one. The human body is a system operating in homeostasis. The American economy, while not an "organism," is so interrelated that changes in a key variable (e.g. investment) will cause determinate changes in other variables (employment, consumption, etc.). Yet in most areas of our lives we do not think in "system" terms. In a city, for example, there will be considerable discussion of the traffic problem, with only the dimmest realization that changes in traffic patterns will have important effects on industry locations, residential densities, and the like—one instance of how rarely we try to scrutinize a problem as a whole.

The Air Force has in the last ten years, for example, had the chastening experience of learning to think not about the production of bombers but about "weapons systems," and the difference is much more than a simple matter of terminology. In deciding what kinds of planes to produce, for example, the Air Force had to take into account such questions as target distances, cruise and dash speeds, bomb loads and yields, alternative ground bases or air refueling, enemy defense performance, enemy offense capabilities, and feasible production schedules; under each of these development variables there were four alternatives, each of which would have affected other aspects of the weapon—the length of landing strips, the size of crews, and so on. Designing a bomber therefore meant having a sense of the entire system in which the weapon was involved.[5]

Similarly, one can think of transportation along the Eastern seaboard, from Boston to Washington, in "system" terms: instead of saving a dying railroad line or building more high-speed roads because more people have cars, the "system" approach calculates how many persons want to travel and how much freight has to be moved over what varying distances, and what combinations of rail, truck, bus, and air vehicles will best serve such diverse needs.

In short, behind all this is an ambitious revolution in conceptual thought. To put it most generally, we tend to think of *entities* but not of *relations, items* but not *contexts; dualities* rather than a *field*. Most of our vocabulary is rich in dualisms like "man and environment," "history and nature," "mind and body," "man and spirit," but we lack *process* terms, which see these relationships as interacting and interpenetrative. When we look at a problem in dualistic terms, we get questions like "How far does environment influence man?" or "How far does man modify his environment?" (the usual answer is "to some extent"), rather than an attempt to examine the question in the unified way of the ecologist—as a biotic community, or as a single analytical system that emphasizes interdependencies and patterned interchanges. By emphasizing relation of events (and not just classes of events), one goes beyond "classical" social analysis, just as modern logic has gone beyhond its Aristotelian foundations.

The final item in this catalogue of the changing importance of "knowledge" is the recent emphasis on research and development.

One can, however, overstate the magnitude of the change. The phrase "research and development" hides many ambiguities, and the customary division into basic research, applied research, and development does not always give a picture of the distribution of money or the value of work done. Thus, the complexity of modern weaponry accounts for much of the stupendous rise in "development" expenditures' and development costs make up more than two-thirds of the total of all research-and-development moneys. A change in accounting methods has also given a new look to what already existed. Thus changes made in 1960 in the budgetary procedures of the Defense Department, the single biggest source of research-and-development funds, greatly expanded the number of things classified under research and development. And in considering simple dollar figures, one has to remember the price inflation from 1940 to the present. Taking all these points into account, David Novick, an economist of RAND Corporation, has stated that the estimated growth in research-and-development funds, in dollar terms, a sixty-fold increase from 1930 to 1958, in real terms should be deflated by half. Even so, the sums are impressive. And so is the number of persons new engaged in research and development. In 1940, about 37,000 persons were engaged in research and development; by 1960, the number had risen to 387,000, a growth rate of more than 10 per cent a year.

In the expansion of research and development, a number of new social trends are evident. Before World War II, most of the research in the United States was underwritten by private industry, but today the basic source of funds is the American government. Given the increasing cost of research—a single experiment by Leon Lederman and

Melvin Schwartz, a Columbia University team, which confirmed the existence of the neutrino, cost a million dollars—only the government would undertake such expenditures. Another crucial point is that while most of the research-and-development money goes into defense, a substantial sum—more than a billion and a half dollars a year for basic research alone—is being spent by the universities, under government contract. This financial fact is transforming the character of the universities as well.

The far-reaching consequences of these social changes are clear: society is becoming "future-oriented," and it is becoming more planned. Planning in this instance, does not mean the centralized direction of the economy from a single source; it is doubtful whether such centralization is even possible in a complex economy. But in simpler and more differentiated ways, planning has already taken hold and will do so increasingly—among individuals planning for careers, corporations and organizations planning future growth and changes, and in a government that tries to anticipate new social needs and to identify future problems.

In step with all this is the growing need for professional and technical skills—and for the expansion of education facilities that train individuals in these skills. The professional and technical employees—the most highly educated of all workers—are, in fact, the faster-growing occupational group in the United States (Table 1). In 1950, almost 5 million persons were employed as professionals and technicians. By 1960, the number rose 50 per cent to 7.5 million. And by 1975 they will number 12.3 million, an increase of almost 65 per cent.

These projections, given in absolute figures, mask some important changes. If we examine these figures for *relative proportions* (Table 2), some interesting perspectives emerge. For one, the semiskilled group, which from 1900 to 1960 went from 12.8 to 18.6 per cent to become the largest single group in the labor force, will begin a relative decline. The proportion of laborers will show a sharp decline. Almost all other groups will about hold their own or gain slightly, but as a proportion of the whole the professional and technical groups will show an appreciably sharp rise.

Table 1: Employment by Occupational Groups: 1960 (actual) and 1975

Total	*1960* *66,700,000*	*1975* *88,600,000*	*Per cent Change (1960-1975)* *33 per cent*
Professional and technical	7,500,000	12,300,000	64
Managers and proprietors	7,100,000	9,600,000	35
Clerical	9,800,000	13,700,000	40
Sales	4,400,000	6,100,000	39
Craftsman and foremen	8,600,000	11,900,000	38
Operatives (semiskilled)	12,000,000	15,500,000	29
Service workers	8,300,000	11,300,000	36
Labourers	3,700,000	3,800,000	3
Farmers and farm laborers	5,400,000	4,400,000	-18

Table 2: Occupational Distribution of Labour Force

(Percent of Total)

Total	*1960* *100 per cent*	*1975* *100 per cent*
Professional and technical	10.8	13.8
Managers and proprietors	10.2	10.8
Clerical	14.5	15.2
Sales	6.5	6.8
Craftsmen and foremen	12.9	13.4
Operatives (semiskilled)	18.6	17.5
Service workers	12.6	12.7
Labourers	6.0	4.2
Farmers and farm labourers	7.9	4.9

It is the professional and technical class, therefore, which becomes the base line for future needs—and educational demands of the society, and the bulk of these are in the scientific, teaching, and health fields (Table 3).

Given the direction of the economy and the weight of

government policy, it is quite clear that in the coming decades the demand for professional and technical personnel will place a considerable burden on the educational system. Take, as one example, the need for scientist and engineers: while the rise of all professional employments will by 1975 be almost *double* the average increase of the labor force, the demand for

Table 3: Professional and Technical Occupations' Makeup (1960)

	Persons
Total	*7,500,000*
Scientific and technical	1,860,000
Engineers	850,000
Technicians and draftsmen	675,000
Scientists	335,000
Teaching	1,775,000
Elementary school	1,000,000
Secondary school	600,000
College and graduate	175,000
Health	1,629,000
Nurses	504,000
Physicians	235,000
Pharmacists	117,000
Dentists	97,000
Health technicians	330,000
Others	350,000
General	2,160,000
Accountants	400,000
Clergymen	250,000
Lawyers	230,000
Musicians and music teachers	175,000
Editors, writers, social workers, designers, etc.	1,000,000

scientists and engineers, as projected, is almost *triple* this average increase. It is estimated that by 1975 we may need as many as 650,000 scientists in the United States, or almost twice as many as in 1960; and over the same period perhaps as many as 2 million engineers, compared to the 850,000 in 1960.

And yet, startling as these projections may be, it is quite likely that by 1975—and perhaps by the year 2000—the need for scientists and engineers can be fancifully looked at in another way. Harrison Brown has sought to demonstrate this by plotting the changing ratio of scientists and engineers to the total population. At the beginning of the century there was one scientist-engineer to about 1,800 persons in the United States. By 1960, the ratio was 1 to 200 (In India, there is one engineer or scientist to every 30,000 persons!). If one extrapolates these trends, by 1980 the ratio would be 1 to every 90 persons, and by the year 2000, 1 to every 40. By comparing this estimate of demand to the curve of supply, Brown concludes that we will need twice as many scientists and engineers as will be available in the year 2000. Or one can take, independently, the computations of the National Science Foundation. They have estimated that there is a 1:2 ratio between the number of engineers and scientists and the expenditures for research-and-development (e.g., from 1954 to 1960, the number of scientists rose 70 per cent while research-and-development funds rose 140 per cent). So far, according to Gilliland panel of the Science Advisory Committee, we are meeting the needs of the next decade, but the "fit" is a tight one.

Now in the health field, there are staggering needs for more physicians, nurses, and other technical personnel. The additional need for more professionals derives from three major factors: the fact that there is an increasing use of medical and hospital services; the change in the patterns of medical practice, as a growing number of doctors devote the greater portion of their time to research rather than to ministering to the sick; and the growth and the changing age distribution of the population. (Today, 17 million persons are between age 55 and 65, and 18 million are 65 and over; by 1975, there will be 20 million persons between 55 and 65, and 21 million of 65 and over). There are in the United States, about 260,000 physicians, and we now graduate 7,500 physicians a year. But this number is not adequate to maintain the *present* physician-population ratio during the next fifteen years (in fact that ratio declined somewhat between 1950 and 1965), and with the increased demand for medical services the number of doctors will have to be expanded.

These projected gaps in scientific manpower suggest a new and unique dimension in social affairs: the economic growth rate in the future will be less dependent on physical capital (money) than it will be on "human capital." And this poses new problems for the society.

In the past, societies moving up the ladder of industrialization required huge sums of money to develop the "infrastructure" (i.e. highways, railroads, canals) and the basic physical plant of heavy industry (steel, energy resources, metals) in order to grow. Today the long-range expansion of the modern economy is limited by the impending shortages of technical and scientific manpower. (One can see this in such a growth area as computer technology, which employs about one-fourth of the 25,000 professional mathematicians in the United States).

The point is obvious, Physical, money capital can be generated rather quickly (as the Soviet Union has shown) by restricting consumption and "sweating" a population. But the planning of human capital is a much more difficult and arduous process. We need to know more about the genetic distribution of brainpower, the means of identifying talent, the procedures for raising I.Q.'s by reshaping home environments, the process of maintaining motivation, and the guidance and husbanding of talent over the long educational process. It means—given the length of schooling—vocational planning on a twenty-five-year cycle.

All of this points up the fact that we are entering a "post-industrial" society in which intellectual achievement will be the premium and in which the "new men" will be the research scientists, mathematicians, economists, *et al.* To say that the basic institutions of the new society will be intellectual is not to say that all or a majority of persons will be intellectuals, engineers, technicians, or scientists. The majority of individuals in contemporary society are not businessmen, yet one can say that this is a "business civilization." The basic values of the society have been embodied in the business institutions; the largest rewards are paid in business.

To say that the major institutions of the new society will be predominantly intellectual is to say, primarily, that the basic *innovative* features of the society will derive not from business as we know it today, principally the "product corporation," but from the research corporations, the industrial laboratories, the experimental stations, and the universities.

This article portrays the knowledge explosion and development of education in historical perspectives.

NOTES

1. These examples are largely drawn from Gerald Holton's "Scientific Research and Scholarship: Notes toward the Design of Proper Scales." *Daedalus* (Spring 1962), pp. 362-99.

2. The National Register is a cooperative undertaking of the National Science Foundation and nine professional scientific societies which in turn work with about 200 specialized societies to produce full listings. Scientists are considered eligible for registration if they have attained the Ph.D. or an equivalent degree in a field of science or have similar qualifications gained in professional experience. A review of the nation's scientific personnel in 1960 brought forth a listing of some 237,000 persons. See the National Science Foundation's *Scientific Manpower Bulletin*, No. 12, 1960, and the descriptive brochure on the National Register, NSF publication 61-46.

3. These are used principally in so-called "queuing" problems, such as the question, in a factory, whether to handle orders on a first-come first-served basis, or wait until different

combinations of order will be built up, or the question of how to plot the best routes and combinations in the shipping of bulk commodities from a wide variety of sources to a large number of different destinations, etc.

4. Oskar Morgenstern, "Limits to the Use of Mathematics in Economics," in *Matahematics and the Social Sciences*, edited by James C. Charlesworth, (Philadelphia, June, 1963).

[*Note*: This article is substantially drawn from the essay of Daniel Bell.]

2

Education: The Intellectual and Moral Revolution

"Morality is a private and costly luxury."

—**Henry B. Adams**

"To give a man full knowledge of true morality, I would send him to no other book than the New Testament."

—**Locke**

Of all periods of human history the genius of man unfolded with greater rapidity and prodigality in the fifth century B.C., commonly called the "Age of Pericles." Almost within one generation were created those marvels of the tragic drama, sculpture, architecture, literature, and oratory that have been looked upon as models for all time. Some of these arts originated in other parts of the Greek world, but the democratic atmosphere of Athens was the environment for their fullest expression.

Athens alone in ancient times provided the right conditions for the evolution of the highest intelligence. Creative thinkers appeared almost everywhere among the Greeks; philosophers and scientists in the coast cities of Asia Minor and also in Megara and Southern Italy; rhetoricians and orators in Sicily; dramatists and historians in various lands. But Athens alone offered them the encouragement and freedom necessary for the full development and expression of their genius. In the long history of that city, just four men were ever persecuted for their radical views.

Athens was the only city where freedom of speech and the grace of eloquence found a home. Until one studies the social, political, moral, and economic conditions of that day it is not possible to appreciate, in any real way, the rise and influence of the higher intellectual and artistic life of man, and to understand their relation to education.

The Persian War which ended in 479 B.C. opened a new era. Previous to this momentous event, the Asiatic tyrants had subjugated the Greeks of Asia Minor, and suppressed the free and full development of life. With the loss of independence, the intellectual and artistic leaderships of the Greeks passed to their Ionian kinsmen in Europe. Athens was not slow in seizing the full advantages of her great victory. In 477 B.C. she formed the Delian league and assumed the treasuryship, thus becoming the head of what was termed a confederacy, but was in fact an extensive and wealthy empire. Her political triumph opened unlimited opportunities for the expression of individual and national ambition, but was unfortunately accompanied by far-reaching changes that began to destroy the fabric of her own inner life.

Political and economic changes. The result of the war was the emergence into leadership of a new class of citizens. Their rise was the result of various causes. First, the Persians had overrun the peninsula of Attica and had devastated the landed estates of the old Athenian aristocracy, impoverishing many of them. Henceforth, the farmers and herdsmen were no longer able to spare the time to go to the city to attend to civic affairs. Second, the soil of Attica, never very fertile, had become depleted, and ceased to be a source of profit. Third, the lower-middle class of people demanded political recognition on the ground that they had won the war. The old aristocracy had been prepared to fight only on land: they had won the celebrated victory of Marathon. The gravity of the struggle with Persia had necessitated the enlistment of all resources, and it was the lower-middle class which manned the Athenian ships that gave the death blow to Asia's might at Salamis. Owing to their splendid naval service, which had been the last hope of the city, the common people claimed a greater share in state affairs. Class struggles, silenced for some time, broke out anew and with increased violence.

As the population of the city grew, the demand arose for the redistribution of civic rights. As a consequence, freemen of every rank and calling, artisans, tradesmen, seamen, and not a few wealthy foreigners, were admitted to citizenship. Many slaves also were freed and enfranchised. Everyone had the right to speak and to vote in the assembly. Leadership came to those who could win the greatest popular applause. The man of eloquence, energy, and resourcefulness readily triumphed over the aristocrat of blood and wealth. Thus Athens became the world's first thoroughgoing democracy.

The consequence was that in Athens, the middle and lower classes tended to monopolize political power.... Of the popular leaders Cleon, the most notorious, was a tanner; another was a baker, another a cattle dealer.... The government of Athens thus became one of political equality imposed upon social inequality. In order that the poor might have opportunity to attend to their civic duties, they were paid for services in the city courts and council. Even attendance at the theatres was paid for at public expense.[1]

Moreover, from a simple agricultural society the Athenians now became a manufacturing and commercial people. Large deposits of clay near the city were used in making fine potteries, for which Athens had become celebrated. About this time, new patterns for decoration of vases came into popularity. Archeologists have unearthed the largest find of Athenian vases in Tuscany, Italy, but they were popular everywhere in the known world. Athens became noted for the manufacturing of arms, cutlery, furniture, and other products. The marble quarries, the silver mines, and other raw materials also played a part in the expansion of commerce and added to the rapidly increasing wealth of the recently enfranchised citizens.

New Social conditions. Under these conditions, as might readily be conjectured, the newly enriched Athenians no longer adhered to the simple and dignified modes of living of bygone days. The number of slaves greatly increased, perhaps up to 150,000. Increased wealth added greatly to the leisure time of citizens, brought luxurious living among the more ambitious, and was not without sinister effects upon the members of the less fortunate classes. Formerly the individual had realized his higher selfhood in service to the state. He had been taught to look upon the performance of his civic duties as the noblest kind of life. Now all this was changed; the majority of citizens preferred paid service in civic office to military service on the field of battle. They soon degenerated into mere lethargic pensioners of the state. Private interests were no longer subordinated to the welfare of the state, but more and more the individual followed his own inclinations and fortunes, regardless of the public good.

Still there was another aspect of the social and political revolution that foreboded ill. The newly enfranchised families from the lower classes did not accept the ideals of strenuous discipline and training to which the aristocratic youth had been subjected. The era of simplicity, uniformity, and rigorous discipline was gone; a new era of complexity and individualism was taking its place. Greater wealth, increased population, and the development of knowledge and technical skill brought about a higher standard of living. Greater refinements along every line required more efficiency in the arts and crafts. Specialization arose, and, as a consequence, technical training became necessary.

Art and literature in the Age of Pericles. The Age of Pericles and the generation following saw the highest development of Athenian art. Phidias, greatest master of sculpture of all times, decorated the Parthenon and the Propylaea with friezes that have never been equaled. The temples, gymnasiums, theaters, and other public buildings of imposing construction, erected in Athens during this period, made it the most beautiful city of the world. Pindar, to the disgust of his fellow Thebans, was inspired to sing:

> O splendid, violet-crowned, glorious Athens,
> Famed in song, pillar of Hellas, city divine.[2]

It was at this time that Aeschylus, Sophocles, and Euripides wrote their superb tragedies. In the following generation Aristophanes produced his comedies; Socrates brought philosophy down from the stars and set it the task of discovering the nature of man; Plato, Xenophon, and Isocrates carried philosophy, literature, and oratory to their highest development; Herodotus and Thucydides wrote their histories; while in the realm of morals, Aesop collected the fables that became the universal text for two thousand years. No other period of time has produced an equal number of men of the first rank of genius in so many fields.

Rise of oratory. The Greeks had always been fond of talking; it may be debated whether they loved sports or wrangling more. As early as the heroic age, the "speaker of words" held the most exalted place in Hellenic regard. With increased leisure the Greeks spent even more time in discussion. Preachers, professors, political campaigners, and public lectures they did not have. Moreover, newspapers and magazines were entirely unknown. Books did not preëmpt attention, for although all citizens could now read, they still preferred the oral to the written word. The living language expressing their vivid sentiments and ideas long continued to dominate attention. Now that democracy had dawned in Athens, oratory had an opportunity to flourish.

The council of war and the panegyric oration delivered in honour of some dead hero may be considered the original sources of oratorical expression. But at least two new conditions tended to raise oratory to the highest development, and to evoke new types of eloquence. First, every man in Athens had to be prepared to speak in his own defense in the courts. Under the restive civic and commercial conditions, every citizen of Athens stood in constant peril of being hauled into court to answer an indictment against him. The readiness with which charges might be preferred against any man by a designing and unscrupulous enemy kept every citizen on the rack. He must be ready to plead his case before his fellow citizens, who acted both as judge and jury. His success depended wholly upon the power of his oratory in persuading the court of his innocence. It must be noted, furthermore, that an Athenian trial was not decided impartially on clear-cut issues of justice and fact; it was rather a question of winning the favor of the jury through an appeal to their emotions. The Athenian juries were large, sometimes composed of five hundred, a thousand, and even fifteen hundred citizens. Under such circumstances, oratorical ability was the essential weapon, both of attack and defense. As Professor Jebb remarks of oratory, "not only was there the most various inducement to cultivate it, but it was positively dangerous to neglect it."

Second, oratory was the one road which led to social and political promotion. In democratic Athens, the prizes of leadership were open to all, but they invariably fell to those who, because of the charm of their eloquence, were more successful in persuading the people to follow their policies. Any citizen could rise on the proper occasionand address the public assembly, but only by the superiority of his eloquence could be hope to have his plans adopted. Athens was the chief state in the world where both sides of public questions were fully debated and the law of the state was adopted by vote of the citizens. Not only was oratory necessary in addressing the public assembly at home, but there were political missions, embassies, and numerous other occasions which appealed to the ambitious. To sum up the causes of oratory, we may borrow the statement of Gomperz:

> The chief instrument of government in practically the whole of Greece was the power of the tongue.... The gift and faculty of speech were the sole road to honor and power. And speech, too, was the sole protection against injustice of every kind. Without

> that weapon a man was exposed to the dangers of hostile attack in his own city, and in times of peace as hopelessly and defenselessly as a warrior without sword or shield on the battlefield. It is not to be wondered at, therefore, that the art of speech should have been cultivated for the first time in the democratic communities of that age as a profession, and that it should have assumed a prominent, if not actually the first place in the education of the young.[3]

Rhetoric as a technical art arose first in Sicily with the establishment of democracy. Corax and Tisias were its originators. The defense of property rights in the courts, after confiscation by the tyrants, furnished the all-sufficient motivation for the special attention to public address. But Athens became the chief center for the cultivation of the new art. Pericles was the first to exhibit its value as a means of political power. Then, too, he brought Cephalus from Sicily to Athens, and Lysias, son of Cephalus, became the first celebrated orator of Greece. It was, however, another Sicilian, Gorgias the sophist, who was the first teacher of rhetoric in Athens. Only in democracy did oratory find the right soil for its fullest development. As a consequence, the pursuit of oratory became the central interest in Greek, culture; and this devotion to speech dominated secondary and higher education for centuries.

Four forms of oratory suitable for various public occasions were distinguished: the *forensic*, concerned with accusation and defense, was used in courts; the *epideictic*, having to do with eulogy or panegyric; the *judicial*, and the *deliberative*, having to do with persuasion and employed especially in public assemblies. Oratorical displays shared with gymnastics the popular enthusiasm at the great national games. The study of oratory, pursued with intense interest, led to the development of various other subjects essential to it.

The beginning of philosophical thought. The disintegration of the fabric of the old Athenian ethos during the fifth century B.C. was due in large measure to the new critical attitude of philosophy and science. The history of education is not directly interested in the numerous cosmological theories that followed each other in rapid succession. It is, however, highly important to understand the circumstances that impelled the leaders in philosophy to pursue those new pathways of thought that led to the higher mental culture, especially as this higher intellectual life became the permanent possession of our race. It will not be denied that some Egyptian and Hebrew sages manifested intimations of philosophic and scientific insight of the first order. The fact, nevertheless, remains that they did not introduce the movement of free intellectual inquiry. The beginning of reflective thought and of the higher mental processes, not only in the individual mind but in the race as such, is of profound concern to genetic psychology and education.

Higher thinking had its origin among the nature philosophers of the Greek cities of Asia Minor. It originated with Thales of Miletus (640-546 B.C.), an Ionian Greek, in the seventh century B.C. Living by the sea and observing the mist forming clouds, he reached the conclusion that rainfall is not caused by some god, but by the natural process of evaporation and precipitation. In this way he substituted natural causation for the mythological or personal causation of the traditional explanation. Henceforth, the Greeks turned to a closer observation of the processes of nature.

Thales was interested in geometry, physics, astronomy, and cosmology. He traveled widely and is reputed to have taught the Egyptians how to calculate the height of a pyramid by its shadow. Other traditions relate that he foretold the eclipse of the sun, and calculated the distance of ships at sea. From observations of many natural phenomena, such as hail and snow, vapor and dew, blood, the juice of fruit, and the deposit of sediment by the river, he concluded that all things have been derived from water.

> These native speculations of Thales are among the great events of human history. A new thing has come into the world, such

> as is not to be found in the ancient homes of civilization, neither in Jerusalem, nor in Babylon, nor in Egypt. The reign of use and wont is over; henceforth men are to base their life on reason. We are standing beside the cradle of newborn thought.[4]

Simple as all this now seems, Thales' view of natural causation was one of the most revolutionary steps in the history of human thinking. He was the first man in recorded history to make scientific deductions from general principles.

Following Thales, the early Greek philosophers were interested mainly in nature and cosmology. They were searching for the elements out of which the external or material world is composed. Other peoples before them had an interest in the varied phenomena of nature, but none of them, so far as we know, had discovered the idea of natural causation.

Now the question—What were the circumstances of Greek thought that brought about the great transition from the idea of personal of mythological causation to natural causation?

The following conditions were chiefly responsible:

(1) The accumulation of large masses of facts in the fields of geography, physics, astronomy, and medicine.

(2) A remarkable psychological readiness in breaking up sensory experiences into component parts.

(3) A society tolerant of variation. The death of Socrates and the exile of several other individuals was the extent of the popular opposition to progressive ideas in Athens. Compared with other peoples, the Greeks were exceptionally tolerant. This spirit of liberality did much to encourage progressive thinking.

(4) An unusual capacity for reintegrating the factors of experience into logical systems of thought. This ability to formulate and systematize ideas in

mathematics, history, and the various sciences, was a new mental phenomenon.

(5) The dissociation of the Greeks from the practical or utilitarian concerns of life and the consequent increase of leisure were further circumstances that favored the emergence of the higher intellectual life.[5]

(6) A sense of causal relation, especially experienced in adapting means to ends. Greek philosophy was based upon the teleological principle.

(7) Unusual power of creative imagination. This quality was shown especially in art. It may well be that the rapid advancement of Greek genius was due primarily to the freedom of art in all its forms.

The causes of the rise of philosophic thought are succinctly stated by a recent humanistic authority, Livingstone, who wrote:

> Athens was in a susceptible, excited mood. At the same time increase of trade brought wealth, and wealth brought emancipation from mean needs, and emancipation brought leisure, and leisure left men free for thought. Finally a democracy was established, in which every citizen took a direct share in the government of his country. Politics became the most important business of life. This latter fact was the immediate cause of the coming of thought.[6]

b. *The progress of science.* The passion of the Greeks for travel in foreign lands and for colonization vastly increased the knowledge of the surface of the earth. At first geography was subsidiary to the study of ethnology and history, but later it came to be a more independent science. The study of history naturally grew out of epic poetry with its stories of the heroes of old. As early as the middle of the sixth century there were numerous writers of history, but, unfortunately, their works have been lost. The science of history culminated finally in the writings of Herodotus, the father of history, and Thucydides, the classic model of historic method.

Mathematics was another science which was undergoing rapid development at this period. Thales of Miletus, first of the seven wise men of Greece, introduced the study of the lines and angles, whereas the Egyptians had dealt primarily with the geometry of surfaces and of solids; the one was empirical and practical in character, the other abstract and scientific. In his measurements of the height of pyramids and the distance of ships at sea, Thales was the first to apply theoretical geometry to practical uses. This abstract and deductive thinking was a new phenomenon in the realm of human culture. Pythagoras (584 or 581 to 500 B.C.) is reputed to have placed a movable bridge under a cord stretched over a resounding board, and by moving the bridge from one end of the cord to the other he demonstrated that tones are governed by definite mathematical laws. This interesting discovery led to a vast amount of investigation into the relation of numbers and to much curious speculation concerning their nature. Pythagoras thought numbers the secret essence of all things. This idea, however fanciful it may now seem, led in time to the application of mathematics to all the fields of physical science.

Before the age of Pericles, the outstanding thinkers directed their attention to the phenomena of nature. Their method was largely speculative, and as a consequence, it soon degenerated into verbal hair-splitting. Nevertheless, considerable progress was made. Xenophanes (540 to ? B.C.) introduced theological criticism and discussed the nature of true being. Empedocles (444 B.C.) proposed a theory of biological evolution. Democritus (460 B.C.) and his disciples propounded the atomic theory of matter, which has been the foundation of physical science to our own time. The range of Greek philosophic interest rapidly broadened, and investigations entered into ever more minute specializations.

But an era of deeper philosophic thought was at hand. In the new era, the problem of education became paramount, and this necessitated the investigation of man's origin, nature, destiny, and the institutions in which he lived.

Henceforth ethics or human relations formed the central theme of philosophic interest. Science had naturally been the concern of a select few. But as ethics, law, government, and education are the proper concern of every man, philosophy became a popular interest.

> In a moment all Athens was seething with this new and revolutionary culture. And further, from the hobby of a few, thought became the property of all, and there sprang up, what otherwise before our own times is unparalleled in history, a thinking nation.[7]

Down to the age of Pericles, the attempts of science were motivated chiefly by practical needs and specific situations, and thinking was guided by empirical processes. Soon, however, the inquiries into the explanation of nature became more abstract. Then, because of its interest in man and human institutions, philosophy became vastly more comprehensive, and thinking was no longer pursued for purely practical purposes. The vivid and powerful imagination of the Greeks led them to dispense with practical considerations as the power that propels thought. Pure intellectual curiosity became the leading motive for investigation. They yearned to know merely for the sake of knowing. Pragmatic thinking or problem solving was superseded by the passion for insight, logical connection, systematic explanation. Knowledge and intelligence had reached its highest level. The Greeks had scaled the heights of rationality and led the race to the highest level of intellectual evolution.

c. *The breakdown of the old morality.* In the progress of every people upward toward higher civilization there comes a time when the old, native morality and traditional customs break down. Such a disintegration is essential before the establishment of life and society upon a higher, broader, and more spiritual basis can take place. In the early period of Athenian culture the people were still in a simple, almost primitive condition. There were five reasons for the breakdown of the old Athenian ethos and character: (1) the traditional theology and the new moral insight were in direct conflict; (2) observation of comparative morals produced a doctrine of relativity; (3) the theory of evolution led to agnosticism; (4) the growth of individualism destroyed social unity; (5) the old education failed to teach civic efficiency. To appreciate how sweeping were the effects of these causes requires a fuller discussion of each.

(1) The traditional Greek religion as presented by the poets was in irreconcilable conflict with the moral ideals that were taught the youth in the home. The poetry which the boy learned by heart pictured the gods and goddesses as engaging in every sort of immoral behavior. They were incestuous, murderous, treacherous, revengeful, intemperate, immodest, and disrespectful to parents. They lied, stole, fought, and lived without law or order. Now the moral training given the young vigorously condemned all such practices. No culture can long endure that imparts one code of morals in its system of education and extols another in the worship of its deities. Heraclitus declared that Homer deserved a sound thrashing for misrepresentation of the gods. This striking contradiction first became intolerable in the time of Plato, but it continued to survive in full vigor for centuries. Lucian, in the second century A.D., described his own experience:

> When I was a boy, what I read in Homer and Hesiod about wars and quarrels, not only of the demigods, but of the gods themselves, and about their amours and assaults and abductions and law suits and banishing of fathers and marrying sisters, I thought all these things were right and I felt an uncommon impulsion toward them. But when I came of age, I found that the laws contradicted the poets and forbade adultery, and theft. So I plunged into great uncertainty, not knowing how to deal with my own case.[8]

To resolve this conflict, Lucian decided to consult the philosophers. On doing so, he learned, to his sorrow, that they were in even greater contradiction in their views of what is right and what is wrong than law and education were with the traditional ideas.

(2) Comparative observation led to relativity of morals and law. Close contact with foreigners at home and travel abroad among races with diverse morals and manners brought about a comparison of moral practices. Such a comparison led first to self-criticism and finally to skepticism. The study of history and ethnology broadened their outlook and added fuel to the fire. The comparative method was ruthlessly applied to the most sacred ideals and traditions. The result was that all social customs, laws, and habits came to be regarded as mere conventionalities of behavior, wholly lacking in authority. In the following tale the historian, Herodotus, presented a striking example of the wide differences in racial behaviour:

> Darius, after he had got into the kingdom, called into his presence certain Greeks who were at hand and asked, "What he should pay them to eat the bodies of their fathers when they died?" To which they answered that there was no sum which would tempt them to do such a thing. He then sent for certain Indians, men who eat their fathers, and asked them while the Greeks stood by and knew by the help of an interpreter all that was said, "What he should give them to burn the bodies of their fathers at their decease?" The Indians exclaimed aloud and bade him forbear such language.[9]

From this, Herodotus concludes that Pindar was correct when he declared "Convention is the king of all men."

The basis of law is the same as that of morals and manners, namely, human invention. In democratic Athens, where the laws were a subject for popular discussion and decision, the validity of laws was subjected to the same criticism as was morality, for in the Hellenic mind generally, moral principles and civil law were identical. More and more as political changes became imperative, the citizen debated, consulted, and voted in the popular assembly, upon all measures of legislation. Thus he came to see that all laws were merely man-made. The only reason for the enactment of any law was that some advantage accrued to the individual or to the state as a whole. If individual or party interest was the sole ground for enacting a law, it was likewise the only reason for obeying it. The Anthenian was all too quick in concluding that the obligation to obey a law extended only so far as it was to his private interest to do so.

If traditional customs and laws were merely human conventions, the problem arose whether there is anything whatever that is valid everywhere and always, any law or moral obligation that is independent of the difference between peoples, states, and times, and therefore, authoritative for all men. This was a search for universal principles of ethics just as science was the search for universal natural laws.

Thus the keen-witted Athenians concluded that as there is no rule of conduct which is necessarily universally binding upon all men, there is nothing that is universally right or wrong. These convictions, which tended to exert a profound influence upon practical life, were accentuated by current evolutionary theories, and by theological skepticism.

(3) The theory of evolution led to agnosticism. The old Greeks had looked upon their laws, their customs, and traditional ideas of right as the direct gifts of the gods; they must be obeyed because their origin carried a divine sanction. But an age of restless innovation, philosophic questioning, and theological speculation naturally scouted this origin. The theories of cosmic evolution of Heraclitus, Anaximander, and Empedocles set up the claim that man had developed gradually from lower forms of life. Anaximander, tracking Thales, derived all things from water; man, he held, sprang from the fish. Such scientific views tended to prove that the farther back one went the less and less perfect were mankind and human institutions. Instead of a golden age in the far past when the gods mingled freely with man and blessed him with divinely revealed truth, there had been merely a condition of primitive savagery. Therefore, the various customs and habits of civilized man were not derived from an all-wise and

divine source, but had come from preceding ages when the race was in a savage or even more primitive condition.

According to Critias, man lived originally without laws just as the animals do. The crude origin of manners and morals, customs and institutions, provoked a feeling of superiority and contempt in the hearts of the aggressive youth. They refused to have their freedom of conduct hampered by the survival of a less enlightened age.

The question of origin always tends to be confused with that of worth and dignity. By teaching the besital origin of man, and the evolution of morals and institutions, naturalistic thinkers destroyed respect for their value and authority. While naturalism was undermining the authority of traditional moral practices, it found a powerful ally in theological criticism. The Greek religion was civic rather than ethical, but nevertheless, obedience to law and moral customs had derived their sanction from the worship of the gods. Athens did not prescribe orthodoxy, but the gods had to be reverenced as a civic duty in order to benefit the city. Rank impiety was thought to bring down their wrath and displeasure.

The deepening ethical sense of fifth-century enlightenment more and more fully perceived the incongruity of primitive polytheism. Among the first to criticize these popular conceptions was Xenophones of Elis, a wandering minstrel and philosopher who preached the unity and purity of the deity with all the enthusiasm of a Hebrew prophet. But his criticisms had more effect than his abstract ideas of the nature of God.

In the next generations the tragic poets, Aeschylus, Sophocles, and Euripides, and philosophers like Plato, advanced the doctrine on monotheism. But in spite of those lofty theological ideals, atheism became widespread. The gods were openly caricatured on the comic stage and became objects of ridicule. Like Diagoras of Melos, who gave utterance to his views in a work termed "Crushing

Speeches," many became ranting and blasphemous atheists. Others took refuge in agnosticism. Protagoras, the first sophist, began his book with this statement; "In respect to the gods, I am unable to know either whether they are or whether they are not, for there are many obstacles to such knowledge, above all the obscurity of the matter, and the life of man in that it is so short." The damaging effects of this open and widespread atheism and agnosticism upon moral conceptions and practices was very great. The religious sanctions of morality became completely shattered.

(4) The growth of individualism destroyed social unity. The brilliant success of the Athenians in the older days was ascribable to the fortunate combination of community will and individual initiative. Community interest, religion, and the patriotic ideal enabled them to present a united front to their enemies without and their problems within. This unity was fostered by the old education that made service to the state the supreme aim of every citizen. Life was still simple, and the subordination of individual interest to the public welfare was the unquestioned rule.

In the era after the Persian War, this *esprit de corps* broke down. Life grew in complexity, and new interests sprang up in great variety. Protagoras taught that man the individual is the measure of all things. The old uniformity lost its charm. Socrates gave impetus to the new tendency by emphasizing the admonition *know thyself.* Patriotism fell to the lowest ebb. Citizens were ready to betray the city for the slightest advantage. Traitors were more admired than despised.

> When men began to ask whether they existed for the good of the state, or the state for their welfare and protection, it was difficult to enforce the demands of patriotism.[10]

One of the reasons for this growth of individualism was the character of Athenian education.

> The spread of education worked in the same direction. The self-development which it proposed as an end was diametrically

opposed to self-devotion for the community, for the more a man's attention was focused on the training of his own powers as an end in itself, the less he was inclined to regard himself merely as one fraction of the state.[11]

Still another cause for the disintegration of Athenian life was the broadening of citizenship and the decrease in the old aristocracy. The new enfranchised lower class with more wealth and less intelligence and moral stamina did not respond to the general will.

Breakdown of the Old Education

The weakness of the old education. The old Athenian education had endeavored to mold the youth into obedient and patriotic citizens, interested in the performance of their duties in war and peace, in public and private. The rapid disintegration of society and of moral conceptions broke down the ideals that had been held up for their admiration.

Not only were the gods immoral; when the light of truth was turned upon the noble heroes of old, they too were far from flawless. Even more than the gods and goddesses these heroes, glorified in song and story, had been held up to youth as moral ideals. Their patriotism, courage, fortitude, and self-control had won freedom for Athens. But, with the growth of individualism, and the evolution of higher morals, these heroic characters no longer retained their glamour for the youth of Athens. With their old ideals shattered, the Athenians were forced to discover new ones around which the character of their youth could be formed. Many suggestions were forthcoming, but none met with universal acceptance. The result was that the youth treated the dignified music and moral training with contempt, and abandoned the rigorous physical culture of the good old days. The old education failed to adjsut in the following ways:

1. Changes in gymnastic took place. The devotion to the traditional ideal of physical training was abandoned, and the youth no longer kept up strenuous exercise.

Athenian gymnastics enjoyed its golden age just prior to the Persian War and for a generation after its close. Pindar (c. 522-443 B.C.) sang his glorious songs in praise of the victors at the great games. Cities vied with one another to honor their successful candidates, and everywhere the most extravagant adulation was paid to the winners. Presents and prizes of all kinds were showered upon the victors, in great contrast to the simple wreaths awarded them in early days.

An enormous change took place in Athenian gymnastics beginning about 440 B.C., strangely coincident with the death of the poet Pindar, who had done more than any other man to celebrate gymnastic prowess. First of all, a distinction arose between gymnastics and athletics. The one pertained to the schools and physical education of boys and youth, the other had to do with training youth and men for winning in the great games. The one aimed at the development of will-power, self-control, and allsidedness. The other aimed only at muscle and brawn trained along some special line such as running, boxing, or wrestling. The testimony of contemporaries agrees that gymnastics suffered a great decline and that athletics were in the ascendency. Euripides (480-406 B.C.) wrote in the *Autolycus.*

Of all the countless evils infesting Greece, there is none worse than the tribe of athletes: first, they neither learn how to live aright, nor could they if they would; how, indeed, when a man is slave to his jaw, and victim to his belly, could he acquire wealth to increase his father's store? Again, they cannot endure poverty, nor adapt themselves to misfortunes.[12]

Aristophanes frequently aimed the shafts of bitter criticism at the decline of interest in the old gymnastic training. In the *Frogs* he complained.

> None has training enough in athletics to run
> With the torch in hand at the races.[13]

. . . . . .

Moreover to prate, to harangue, to debate, is now the ambition of all in the state,

Each exercise ground is in consequence found deserted and empty.[14]

Socrates noted a lack of interest in gymnastics[15] and thought that specialization was overdoing the growth of the legs of the runners, and the trunk and arms of boxers. Xenophon watched the change in physical education with utter disgust, deplored the drift away from sound physical training, and the scornful attitude of youth:

The spirit of beautiful and brave manhood has taken wings and left our city. . . . When will he pay as strict attention to the body who is not content with neglecting a good habit, but laughs to scorn those who are careful in the matter![16]

The unknown author of *The Constitution of Athens*, evidently exaggerated the situation when he wrote:

Citizens devoting their time to gymnastics and to the cultivation of music are not to be found in Athens; the sovereign people has disestablished them, not from any disbelief in the beauty and honour of such training, but recognizing the fact that these are things the cultivation of which is beyond its power.

Besides this they are given shoes to wear which tend to make their feet tender, and their bodies are enervated by various changes of clothing. And as for food, the only measure recognized is that which is fixed by appetite.[17]

The degeneration of physical stamina affected their clothing as well. The youth no longer contented themselves with the simple, sleeveless chiton but began to wear overcoats. The disastrous effects of this softening became evident when the Athenian soldiers were decisively beaten by the warriors of conservative Sparta.

Plato distinguished between gymnastics and athletics,

and pointed out that all athletes became brutal and sluggish. He laid the blame upon society.

At the time of the Persian War, Athenian citizens, young and old, rich and poor, enthusiastically pursued gymnastic training. By the time of the Pelophonnesian conflict few, if any, were willing to subject themselves to the strenuous activities of the gymnasium. That the change set in about 440 B.C. is attested by the scenes depicted by the paintings on their pottery. The artists had ceased to show the youth engaging in the toils of gymnastics, but portrayed them lounging around and engaging in discussion.

What brought about these changes? Many suggestions have been forwarded by ancient and modern students:

a. Aristophanes laid the blame for the change to love of luxury and effeminacy. The youth forsook the hard exercises for warm baths, horse racing, and dancing girls.

b. More palaestrae were required and these were built in luxurious style and ornamentation.

c. In former times all adults except the officials were forbidden to enter the palaestra and mingle with the boys and youth. This precaution was neglected, and the men used the opportunity for degrading practices. Parents of delicate feelings shielded their sons from these abuses as much as they could, but they continued to flourish nevertheless.

d. Professionalization had an evil effect. As the rules became more strict, gymnastics became increasingly more technical and professional. Only those who followed the special training could hope for victory in the celebrated games.

e. From being the sport of gentlemen, gymnastics became the art of making money. Bribery was common. Victory was for sale. Olympia was free for a long time from such commercialism, but in 338 B.C. the practice of bribery began even there.

f. Gymnastic training was no longer sought as a preparation for military fitness. More and more, the army was recruited from mercenary soldiers. Young men preferred the enjoyments of life at home to the toils of war.

g. The most important reason for the lack of interest in gymnastics was that the enthusiasm of Athenian youth had found a new object of devotion. The heroes who attracted the greatest adulation at the end of the fifth century B.C., and for years to come, were the Sophists and teachers of rhetoric. No one can read the story of Protagoras in Athens[18] without discovering that a new era was opening. While the interest in intellectual culture was not universal among the youth, its appeal to the best of them was all-powerful.

2. The second reason for the failure of the old education was that the youth disregarded its moral precepts and practices. Young men no longer believed in the gods or revered the national heroes. They ceased to show proper respect for parents and elders, and became extravagant, licentious, and unruly. They frequented the market place and the baths, and spent much time in gambling, or in debauchery with ballet girls. Horse racing, cock fighting, and feasting became daily occupations. Plato lamented the decline of civic virtue:

Here at Athens there is a dearth of commodity, and all wisdom seems to have emigrated from us. . . . I am certain that if you were to ask any Athenian whether virtue was natural or acquired, he would laugh in your face, and say: Stranger, you have far too good an opinion of me; if I were inspired I might answer your question. But now I literally do not know what virtue is, and much less whether it is acquired by teaching or not.[19]

Another witness to the failure of the old education to perpetuate virtue in the youth was Aristophanes the poet. In his comedies, he contrasted the old with the new and severely censured the degeneration of morals and manners. He represented the old education as pleading with the youth to choose the good old ways:

> But now must the lad from his boyhood be clad
> In a Man's all-enveloping cloak:
> So that, oft as the Panathenaea returns,
> I feel myself ready to choke
> When the dancers go by with their shields to their thigh,
> not caring for Pallas a jot.
> You therefore, young man, choose me while you can;
> cast in with my Method your lot;
> And then you shall learn the forum to spurn,
> and from dissolute baths to abstain,
> And fashions impure and shameful abjure,
> and scorners repel with disdain:
> And rise from your chair if an elder be there,
> and respectfully give him your place,
> And with love and with fear your parents revere,
> and shrink from the brand of Disgrace,
> And deep in your breast be the Image impressed
> of Modesty, simple and true,
> Nor resort any more to a dancing-girl's door,
> nor glance at the harlotry crew,
> Lest at length by the blow of the Apple they throw
> from the hopes of your Manhood you fall.[20]

3. Changes of a radical character took place in music. The use of the flute with its more piercing and stimulating notes became popular and rivaled the cithara. New songs with new rhythms were introduced. For the first time, poetry became subordinate to melody, and then arose music completely unaccompanied by words.

Whereas formerly the poet composed his own melody, was entire master of his chorus, and was the recipient of all the glory won by the performance, it is now the bandmaster, who is all important, while the poet is a mere verse-writer who receives his orders from the musician as from a superior.[21]

These changes in music called forth the scathing denunciation of Aristophanes, Plato, and many others. Plato declared that the change in music had subverted the laws and the moral foundations of the state.

But out of the old education in music-poetry-dancing came a new evil, panatomimicry. It will be recalled that the Athenian education originally aimed at all-sidedness and abhorred specialization. With the expansion of personal interests and the training in dramatization, all-sidedness led to charlatanry. It produced good speculators, historians, dramatists, and artists, but poor generals, statesmen, and businessmen. Efficiency and skill require specialization of training. The dislike of specialization and the lack of specific technical training produced the jack-of-all-trades and master-of-none. The Athenians carried their versatility to an absurd extreme. Juvenal satirized this aspect of their culture:

> A Protean tribe, one knows not what to call,
> Which shifts to every form, and shines in all:
> Grammarian, painter, augur, rhetorician,
> Ropedancer, conjurer, fiddler, physician,
> All trades his own your hungry Greekling counts:
> And bid him mount the sky—the sky he mounts!
> No longer now the favourites of the stage
> Boast their exclusive power to charm the age;
> The happy art with them a nation shares,
> Greece is a theatre, where all are players.
> For lo! their patron smiles—they burst with mirth;
> He weeps—they droop, the saddest souls on earth;
> He calls for fire, they court the mantle's heat;
> 'Tis warm, he cries—and they dissolve in sweat.[22]

This versatility of expression became the chief weakness of Greek moral character. They were altogether too imitative and consequently lacked stability, integrity, and loyalty to principle.

4. The final weakness of the old education was in its failure to meet the expanding needs of the new age. As long as Athens remained small and retained the old simplicity of

life, the former education was sufficient. But in the expansion of the state better technique was necessary to keep in line with the expansion of knowledge and improvement of professional and technical skills.

Such were the general conditions of philosophy, social life, and education in Athens, and indeed throughout all democratic Greece, during the latter half of the fifth century B.C. Old customs and institutions, fast crumbling under the fierce attacks of criticism, no longer exercised a restraining influence over the conduct of the individual. How to better these degenerate conditions formed a complicated problem whose solution challenged the powers and genius of their greatest minds.

New educational needs. The standard of living had risen in Athens, and the most elaborate needs of practical and civic life could no longer be met by the crude technique of untrained men, however clever and resourceful they might naturally be. When every art from taking a walk to cooking a dinner was made a subject of critical investigation, technical performance could not remain in a primitive condition. Generalship of the army, leadership of the navy, diplomacy, and all the other offices of government and social life had to be filled by men who not only were possessed of intelligence, but who were likewise equipped with expert knowledge and skill in performance. The elementary education in gymnastics, music, reading, and writing did not equipment for the demands of these specialized professions. The increased intellectual activity and higher technical performance demanded expert training.

All citizens sit in parliament; every office from commander-in-chief to civil-service clerk is open to talent; an aristocrat, a grocer, an artisan may equally become premier: he has only to persuade parliament to elect him. In such a state the first need is a gift of speech: an eloquent, plausible, convincing tongue. That is the one road to power. With it a man may achieve anything. Only, where can he learn the art of speaking, and, what is more important than speech, the art of knowing what to say? If we can conceive of a nation in this plight, we shall know what athens was like after the Persian wars.[23]

Public speaking, whether to the assembly, the jury, or on any other occasion, demanded a knowledge of rhetorical technique and a logical mode of approach. Beauty of speech and correctness of language and thought required training along lines which had never been known before.

To meet the urgent needs of the new age, a threefold educational demand sprang up: There was needed (1) a more definite training in the higher field of general culture; (2) an urgent demand for new information and increased skill, especially in the language arts and in all the technical sciences; and (3) a more comprehensive philosophy of the world and of man that would include within it a sound philosophy of education.

The new educational opportunity. Under the old Athenian education, the youth, having completed elementary training in the schools of the grammatist, the citharist, and the paidotribe, had no opportunity to learn anything that would help him in the technical and professional vocations. No provision had been made in Athens either by private parties or by the state for secondary or higher training of a cultural and professional character.[24] Various individuals now began voluntarily to fill this gap in the educational life of the times by teaching the youth and young men to think, speak, and act more efficiently in all private and public affairs.

The relaxing of the practice of gymnastic training, and also of civic and military duties, afforded the youth plenty of leisure for such intellectual pursuits.

Advancement of Learning and the Sophists

A. Gomperz says, "Half-professor and half-journalist— that is the best formula that we can devise," to characterize the sophists of the fifth century B.C." The number of these individuals was small, and only one of them could claim Athens as his native city. Owing, however, to its wealth, culture, and literary patronage Athens became the favorite resort for these peripatetic instructors. They did not attempt to set up permanent schools even in Athens, choosing rather to wander from city to city as the rhapsodists of old who were their cultural predecessors.

The term "sophist" was employed in a loose way to designate any man who was wise or clever along any line. In this sense it was used to include men of practical wisdom, such as Solon, and likewise the teachers of nature philosophy; by some it was also applied to Socrates. Later the term was given a narrower significance referring particularly to the teachers of rhetoric and ethics who during the latter half of the fifth century began to accept money for their instruction. A closer view of these early teachers and their instruction is necessary because of their great educational contributions.

PROTAGORAS

The earliest and most renowned of the new teachers of Athens was Protagoras (c. 490 B.C.) of Abdera, in Thrace. He came to Athens in 445 B.C. under the patronage of Pericles. Observing that the need of the hour was greater efficiency in the performance of public and private affairs, he set himself up as an instructor along these lines. He claimed that from his instruction a student would acquire:

> Prudence in affairs private as well as public; he will learn to order his own house in the best manner, and he will be able to speak and act for the best in the affairs of the city.[25]

In other words, Protagoras professed to make good citizens; men who would be successful in private affairs, and efficient in public service. It is interesting to discover that this first popular teacher reflected carefully upon the art of education, and wrote a book on pedagogy, several principles of which still remain. These principles are as follows: "Teaching requires natural disposition, and exercise, and must be begun in youth." "Neither theory without practice nor practice without theory avails at all." "Culture does not flourish in the soul unless one reaches a great deepness."

Another book, *On Correct Speech*, marks him as the first investigator of grammar, a subject which he not only originated but introduced into the curriculum. Wherever he taught, he met with enormous success, and his popularity with the young men of Athens was phenomenal. Protagoras may well be regarded as the father of secondary education and one of the greatest educational innovators. According to Diogenes Laertius he was the first:

1. To teach as a Sophist in Athens,
2. To maintain that there are two sides to every question,
3. To distinguish the tense of verbs,
4. To institute contests in debating,
5. To teach rival pleaders the tricks of their trade,
6. To exact a fee of a hundred minae,
7. To point out how to attack and refute any proposition laid down,
8. To mark off the parts of discourse into four, namely, *wish, question, answer, command.*[26]

PRODICUS OF CEOS (465-399 B.C.)

After Protagoras, Prodicus was the most prominent teacher. He professed to impart civic efficiency, that is, virtue and good character. He laid emphasis especially upon practical ethics, and his parable, the *Choice of Hercules,*[27] was very popular for moral instruction. In addition to morals, he taught nature philosophy, the history of religions, and gave great attention to the right use of language. *He was the first man to draw up lists of synonyms and antonyms.* The historian, George Grote, vigorously defended Prodicus' effort to bring greater accuracy into the use of words:

Prodikus, again, published one or more treatises intended to elucidate the ambiguities of words;... the purpose was one pre-eminently calculated to aid Grecian thinkers and dialecticians; for no man can study their philosophy without seeing how lamentably they were hampered by enslavement to the popular phraseology, and by inferences founded on mere verbal analogy. At a time when neither dictionary nor grammar existed, a teacher who took care, even punctilious care, in fixing the meaning of important words of his discourse—must be considered as guiding the words of his hearers in a salutary direction.[28]

Though he emphasized precision in the use of language, ethics nevertheless was his uppermost interest.

HIPPIAS OF ELIS

Hippias was the most versatile and bombastic of these early professors, and the first of the Greeks to aim at universalism in knowledge. On one occasion he appeared at the Olympian games clothed from head to foot in apparel made by his own hand, "from sandals on his feet to the plaited girdle round his waist and the very rings on his fingers." He proudly courted notoriety as a jack-of-all-trades. He offered to give instruction in all branches of learning as well as in the fine and professional arts. Possessing the type of mind that undertakes to popularize knowledge, he gave superficial training in astronomy, geometry, arithmetic, poetry, grammar, politics, and archaelogy. He aimed to make his students ready debaters along every line and on both sides of any question.

As a creative scholar, he wrote on phonetics, rhythm and music. He produced theories of sculpture and painting. His system of mnemonics was remarkably successful. When an old man, it is stated, he was able by its aid to retain fifty new names heard for the first time without omitting or misplacing a single one. He proved his versatility by writing tragedies, epics, epigrams, and dithyrambs. He compiled a list of Olympic victors, composed a collection of memorable events, wrote a work on national names, and made some contribution to geometry.

GORGIAS OF LEONTINI (C. 473-375 B.C.)

Gorgias made no claim to teaching civic efficiency or virtue. His one aim was rhetoric, and he preferred to be called *rhetor* rather than sophist. He had studied under Tisias, the Sicilian orator, and came to Athens as head of an embassy in 427 B.C. His fame rests on two things: he was the first Greek writer to use prose in place of poetry; he also introduced the technical study of rhetoric into Athens. Gorgias was particularly interested in beauty of expression. Jebb states, "Gorgias was the first man who definitely conceived how literary prose might be artistic."

B. The attitude of the Sophists to the moral problem of Athens may be summed up in four points.

1. They believed that pleasure is the *summum bonum* which every man seeks, and they were quite incapable of conceiving of any higher or better goal for human desire. They held that the interest of the individual lies in controlling his actions in order to experience as many pleasant sensations as possible. Furthermore, they held that the interests of the individual are more important than the welfare of the state. The old civic ideal had lost its power over the individual will, and was replaced by a goal that did not lead to strenuous exertion, but only to sensuous inaction.

2. Conduct motivated by spontaneous impulse was considered superior to the conduct that merely imitated traditional morals. Nature was sharply contrasted with convention, as it was later in eighteenth-century Europe. Since prevailing moral sanctions had fallen into desuetude, there was no adequate reason why natural impulses should be

restrained or controlled. The Sophists failed to see that spontaneous impulses must always be guided by some higher principle in the interest of a social ideal. If there is no such larger imperative, there is no reason for the government and discipline of the irrational life of appetite and impulse.

3. It logically followed that there could be no fixed principles of right and wrong. If pleasure is the measure of value, that is, of the good, then the individual becomes the measure of the ethical world. What gives him pleasure is the right thing for the moment. It may be wrong at another time for him and may be right or wrong for others. What is bitter to one might be sweet to another. It is a mere matter of individual feeling. Consequently there is no absolute right or wrong for everybody and for all times. In other terms, the sophistic teaching denied the universality of ethical principles. Right and wrong became mere matters of individual taste and had utterly lost any general significance. This conclusion involved the logical destruction of moral life. The individualism of the Greeks had reached its climax in theory as well as in practice.

4. Corresponding to the exaltation of impulse in the ethical sphere was their doctrine of sensation in the intellectual sphere. They believed that the sensations of the individual are the criteria of truth. Consequently there is no universal truth, but all is relative to the perception of the moment.

C. There was need of a new accurate knowledge. Athens was seething with new energy, but technical knowledge did not match the burgeoning arts and complex activities of life. This need of new knowledge of all sorts was keenly felt. Without newspapers, magazines, the lecture platform, the pulpit, the college classroom, and the laboratory, the means that supply the intellectual and emotional life in our day, the Hellenic world had to find some substitute. That substitute was supplied by the Sophists who became the investigators and teachers of the time. However, before they could instruct to advantage, they were obliged to investigate and discover the basic facts of the various fields, for the materials for training in the higher professions were still lacking. Thus these men became not only the first professors of higher learning but also the first research professors.

1. Precision of thought produces study of language. The culture of the Greeks had grown out of religion and folklore as expressed in poetry and music. Down to the time with which we are now dealing, all literature was in the poetic form. Now, as every one knows, poetry is emotional, imaginative, and notoriously lacking in precision of thought. The critical study of science and philosophy naturally brought poetical language into disrepute. Under the spur of the need for greater precision and exactness of thought and expression, interest in language became dominant. Democratic conditions necessitating the study of oratory still further accentuated the attention to language arts. An investigation into the nature of language became inevitable. The loose terminology of the former era had to give way before the more exact and logical thinking of the new age. Scientific grammar, etymology, syntax, the laws of rhetoric, the rules of logic, and, finally, the origin of language became matters of profound study. Language is at once the vehicle of thought and its treasury. The conquest of all phases of language was, therefore, essential before the human mind could make the steep ascent to the highest level of intelligence, that is, to positive knowledge. These investigations into language and the teaching of the language arts were not the work of any one man, but of many independent scholars.

Grammar. It is a curious circumstance in the history of language that no one had the slightest knowledge of grammar until this time. Innumerable languages had grown up, and great literary works had been composed, though not a single author distinguished a noun from a verb. What is still more curious, fine distinctions were made by the use of different verbal forms to show tense, number, and mood without any consciousness on the part of men that they were making such distinctions. It is evident that the use of different forms to express variations in meaning is independent of any conscious knowledge of rules. Just so children acquire the use of the tenses long before they make any conscious analysis of the grammatical forms involved.

Grammar as the scientific knowledge of the use of language began with Protagoras. He was the first man to call attention to the use of different forms of words to express masculine, femine, and neuter gender. He also distinguished the moods and tenses in the use of verbs and also the different forms of address. He formulated some rules of correct speech and even attempted to reform some traditional usages. Later Plato and others made additions to grammatical knowledge. At any rate the scientific analysis of language began at this time—a development that owned its inception to the deepening insight of the human mind in all fields of thought, and an outgrowth of a need for more definite and exact thought and expression.

Rhetoric and oratory. The development of interest in rhetoric and oragory at the end of the fifth century B.C. in democratic Greece was one of the most important movements in human culture. Soon these subjects were to become the heart of the curriculum, and language began to dominate the school room. Protagoras invented the use of themes on which his students wrote arguments both pro and con. His aim was to train the pupil's keenness of wit and dexterity in argument; at the same time to equip him with a stock of ideas and phrases to be kept in constant readiness for use. Prodicus wrote a book, *On Correct Language.* This work has not come down, and we do not know what aspects he treated. But we do know that in collecting and comparing synonyms so as to distinguish their shades of meaning, he was calling attention to one of the greatest needs of the day. Exact thought could make no progress until language was a sharper and more effective instrument of expression.

In an age of pioneer investigation, ambiguity is always one of the chief faults of all philosophical, ethical, and scientific thinking. It causes interminable discussion and disagreement of opinions. A special need of the effervescent fifth century was that of a dictionary. To make up for this lack, the Sophists and Socrates and Plato devoted themselves assiduously to the classification and definition of words.

However, not only clearness and accuracy of thought were sought; beauty of expression also was desired. Gorgias made oratory a matter of study and instruction. As was but natural, at first oratory and prose style retained many of the characteristics of poetry. The teaching of rhetoric and oratory to young men who were eager for instruction naturally followed the new need for skill in public speech. In this, Gorgias the foreigner became leader.

Received with acclamation he spent the rest of his long life in central Greece winning applause by the display of his oratorical gifts and acquiring wealth by the teaching of rhetoric.[29]

The prose style of Gorgias was decidedly of the florid type. The study of grammar, rhetoric, and oratory was closely connected with the study of rhythm, meter, phonetics, and the theory of harmony. The Greek passion for beauty of expression which was formerly confined to poetry was now transferred to oratorical displays.

In general, the Sophists aimed to train the youth to speak, to think, and to act effectively in private and public affairs. Seeing that by tradition morals and manners had been the dominant objective in training, it was entirely natural that the Sophists should set themselves up as the new teachers of virtue or civic efficiency. Their instruction comprised a vast range of subjects: the elements of the positive sciences; the theories of the nature philosophers; the interpretation and criticism of poetry; the rudiments of grammar, etymology; the elements of arithmetic, geometry, astronomy, geography, natural history; the laws of meter, rhythm, history, mythology, genealogies, politics, ethics; criticism of religion, mnemonies, tactics and strategy, music and harmony, drawing, painting, scientific athletics, political science, archaeology, physics, administration of the household and of government, and, above all, rhetoric and argumentation. No one sophist gave instruction in all lines, but, since knowledge was not systematized, each man followed his own interests.

In this labor of instruction and investigation, the Sophists offered courses of instruction, ordered the materials, and elaborated the sciences. These men formed in a loose sort of way the first European university. By the nature of the situation they were at once investigators into the different fields of knowledge and instructors of youth.

The young men of Athens were filled with abounding enthusiasm for the new instruction. Higher learning for the first time had cast its spell upon mankind. They were impelled by an irresistible impulse for intellectual inquiry and gladly paid enormous fees for the privilege of learning from these men, the first professional teachers of the Greek world.

A fierce conflict of opinion has raged in regard to the influence of the Sophists upon the moral life of the time. Of their writings nothing has survived but a few quotations. Our knowledge of them has come from their bitter enemies, the traditionalists on the one hand, and the idealistic reformers on the other. The chief charges against them were these: they taught for money, a gross offense against the ethical sensibilities; they were superficial, pretentious, ambitious, bombastic; and they taught the young men skill in argumentation—a skill which was as readily used to defend falsehood and evil as the true and good. However, be it said to their credit, they ministered to the intellectual needs of the times, and while their ethical philosophy may have been superficial and misleading, their intellectual and aesthetic instruction was salutary and in accord with popular needs. To them we owe the introduction of secondary and higher intellectual education.

SOCRATES

Personality. Socrates—what a name that had been to conjure with! For upward of twenty centuries synonym of wisdom and philosophy, and the world's ideal sage. What a brain he had! What inexhaustible stores of mental energy!

One morning he was thinking about something which he could not resolve; he would not give it up, but continued thinking from early dawn until noon—there he stood fixed in thought; and at noon attention was drawn to him, and the rumour ran through the wondering crowd that Socrates had been standing and thinking about something ever since the break of day. At last, in the evening after supper, some Ionians, out of curiosity (I should explain that this was not in winter, but in summer), brought out their mats and slept in the open air, that they might watch him and see whether he would stand all night. There he stood all night until the following morning; and with the return of light he offered up a prayer to the sun and went his way.[30]

Twenty-four hours or more of sustained and profound thinking!

In personality Socrates was one of the two most unique figures in human history. Physically he was ugly, almost repulsive. His nose was broad with wide spreading nostrils; his lips thick, his eyes protruding. His figure was portly, and he walked with a waddle. He went about with bare feet and his garment was old and slovenly and full of holes. To the beauty-loving Greeks, he strongly resembled a Satyr. Believing as they did that beautiful souls are found only in beautiful bodies, his fellow citizens concluded that Socrates must be exceedingly depraved. But he was reputed for his courage and his great physical endurance. As a rule he was abstemious to the extreme in eating and drinking; nevertheless, occasionally he was known to drink everyone under the table, without the least symptom of intoxication.

Life and vocation. This remarkable figure was born in Athens in 469 B.C. His parents were too poor to give him the regular education of a gentleman. Naturally he learned to read and write, but he missed the ordinary training in music and dancing. What further instruction he received is uncertain, though it is claimed that he was taught the nature sciences of the day. Following in the footsteps of his father, at an early age he took up sculpture as a vocation.

Socrates performed the ordinary duties of a citizen with conscientious efficiency. He acted as soldier and juror, and regularly attended the public assembly in which he once served as president. But an inner voice warned him against any special political ambition. He married and became the father of three sons, but his family relations were by no means happy. It is, however, unjust to lay too much of the blame upon Xantippe, for men of great genius are often hard to live with, and the eccentricities of Socrates must have been especially irritating.

When the under what circumstances Socrates deserted sculpture and turned to teaching we are not informed. At his trial he declared he was divinely commissioned to teach.[31] And when confronted with the alternative of quitting his teaching or being condemned to death, he cheerfully chose to die rather than give up his vocation. Socrates was the world's greatest educational martyr. To him the satisfaction of teaching and of pursuing clear ideas far outweighed the loss of life.

One must not picture Socrates as a professional instructor lecturing in the conventional ways. The circumstances were otherwise; he went about Athens in an informal manner ever alert to find someone whose ideas needed correcting and enlarging or whose conduct or technique needed expert guidance. In the morning he usually went to one of the palaestrae; at noon he mingled with the crowd at the market place; and the afternoon he spent in one of the gymnasia or some other place where men congregated in numbers. But wherever he went, he engaged some individual in discussion and plied him with question after question, seeking as he sincerely avowed, to discover accurate information. He always contended that he did not know anything himself. In questioning others he soon involved them in hopeless contradiction and confusion. But in all the discussions and wrangling, his one aim was to direct the youth to virtuous life, and to reach clear conceptions. In an age of insatiable curiosity, Socrates was the foremost inquirer, for he was possessed by a profound passion for the investigation of clear, universal ideas. For thirty years or more he pursued this strange mode of life.

The disciples of Socrates. In his peripatetic instruction, Socrates talked with all classes of people. Naturally he did not treat them all alike, but fitted his dialectic discussion to the needs of each individual. The students he prized most were those who had "a readiness to learn," "power of retaining," and who possessed self-control and an ambition to excel in practical affairs.

Young men of all classes of society sought his counsel and attended his steps to hear his discussions. Thus he was generally accompanied by a group who hung upon his words and became his constant followers. Some of these went forth to practice his quizzing method upon others, to their bitter disgust. These came to harbor a deep hatred against the master, believing that his influence upon the youth was bad. Among his followers were many who became famous as teachers, thinkers, and statesmen. One thinks first of Plato, Xenophon, Euclid of Megara, and Isocrates.

The Socratic Doctrines. a. *Field of thought.* The

subjects that claimed the exclusive attention of Socrates and that invariably formed the topic of his discussion had to do with the art of living, or human relations. The virtues, such as justice, temperance, courage, gratitude, and friendship; also, the nature of wealth, statesmanship, and question concerning government, the practical arts and crafts, and household economy exhausted the range of his inquiries. According to Xenophon, one of his most ardent followers,

> He never wearied of discussing human topics. What is piety? What is impiety? What is the beautiful? What the ugly, What the noble? What the base? What are meant by just and unjust? What by sobriety and madness? What by courage and cowardice? What is a state? What is a statesman? What is a ruler over men? What is a ruling character? and like problems.[32]

Socrates did not attempt any investigations into physics or biology. By their many contradictions, the nature philosophers had led students into hopeless confusion. For this reason Socrates came to believe that the gods had intentionally hidden the secrets of nature from human knowledge. Theology, also, failed to attract him. The limitation of his intellectual horizon was due to his special interests as an investigator and teacher. Man and human institutions were his sole field of inquiry. Subjects that had significance for the education of the youth were of peculiar interest, for Socrates was primarily an educational philosopher. The fact was, he recognized that education was man's supreme problem, and that this problem required a clarification of the virtues that constituted the aim of education. Of old, it had been said that he brought down philosophy from heaven; this simply meant that he substituted investigation of the problems of every day life for the airy, cosmological speculations of the nature philosophers.

b. *Socrates' view of the curriculum.* Xenophon has left a short discussion of Socrates' ideas of pedagogy. He believed in gymnastics, especially for the sake of health, sanity, and military efficiency. Dancing, music, and poetry he recommended for the development of the personality of the true gentleman. Practical religion, but not theology, had a large place in his informal course; for Socrates was a man of genuine piety. Geometry was to be taught so far as it had practical application, astronomy for its value in forecasting the seasons and keeping track of time. Arithmetic was approved for business reasons. Psychology, too, won his favor; self-knowledge was, of all subjects, most essential for the attainment of happiness; and last and most important was ethics or the science of the virtues.

Great as was his thirst for knowledge, Socrates avowed no interest in knowledge for its own sake. But he firmly believed in freedom of inquiry. For inquiry, he declared, at his trial, "I am ready to fight, in word and deed, to the utmost of my power." Only those subjects, or those aspects of a subject, that had a practical bearing upon life found favor in his sight. For the general theory and insight into the nature of the world and man he cared nothing. Knowledge necessary to administer one's private affairs, to run the state, to produce goods efficiently, and to live a temperate, just, and happy life constituted the course of Socratic teaching. He was the first great leader in the field of the pragmatic theory of education.

c. *Discovery of universal elements in knowledge.* "Two things," said Aristotle, "may be ascribed to Socrates, inductive reasoning and the fixing of general concepts." The main object of Socrates was to introduce clear thinking into the intellectual life of Athenian society. "He thirsted for pure concepts as ardently as may mystic ever panted for union with the God-head," declares Gomperz. We have already seen the confused condition of contemporary intellectual life. It was purely on the sensory and empirical level of development. Since his day, the establishment of higher patterns of thought, the development of true concepts, the defining of terms, has been the prodigious labor of students for centuries. Socrates was the first to show the necessity for such clarity in thought, and to demonstrate the only method by which it could be obtained. He confined himself to the search for clear concepts in the fields of ethics; his purpose was to clarify the ideas of the virtues so as to secure a more efficient ethical life.

The identification of knowledge and virtue. "No man errs of his own free will." This was the fundamental tenet of the Socratic philosophy. All error is due solely to ignorance. If a man knows what is right, he will do what is right. No one will voluntarily and intentionally do wrong. This is a highly plausible theory. Let us trace the course of his reasoning as it is presented in the *Protagoras* of Plato.

First, it is asserted that pleasure is the only good. Now it is axiomatic that all men seek happiness, and that only the good are happy. Furthermore, happiness consists of those things that bring pleasure, provided they are not later attended by consequences that produce plain.

In every act, men seek what they consider is the good, *i.e.*, that which will produce pleasure. If, perchance, it turns out that the chosen line of conduct leads to painful consequences that were not foreseen, then this line of conduct was pursued ignorantly. If a man can foresee all the remoter results which are inevitably connected with a choice, he will undoubtedly select only the good, that is to say, only those actions that produce permanent pleasure. Men, therefore, choose evil and engage in conduct that brings undesirable consequences because of ignorance. To know the right, to think it clearly, vigorously, and comprehensively, is to perform it; on the other hand, to think and know, in the truest sense, the wrong, the evil, to have a farsighted and steady vision of its consequences is to reject and avoid it. Therefore, knowledge, real knowledge and sound judgment, will always lead to virtuous conduct, which ignorance, on the other hand, is the cause and synonym of evil. This thought is clearly expressed in Plato's *Protagoras*:

O, Protagoras and Socrates, what is the meaning of being overcome by pleasure if not this?—tell us what you call such a state—if we had immediately and at the same time answered "Ignorance" you would have laughed at us. But now, in laughing at us you will be laughing at yourself; for you also admit that men err in their choice of pleasures and pains; that is, in their choice of good and evil, from defect of knowledge; and you admit further, that they err not only from defect of knowledge in general, but of that particular knowledge which is called measuring. And you are aware that the erring act which is done without knowledge is done in ignorance.[33]

How did Socrates come to reach such a conception? Before entering upon a discussion as to whether Socrates' conception of the relation of knowledge and virtue is true or false, let us inquire how he came to accept it.

First, as Gomperz points out, "Socrates possessed an ideal—an ideal of calm self-possession, of justice, of fearlessness, of independence. He felt that he was happy because, and in so far as, he lived up to this idea." Here is the fact of highest importance: there was no vacillation in his aim. He had a profound sense of the ideal life, and in pursuing it he tolerated no compromises.

Second, Socrates was a man of balanced temperament; the poise and harmony of all elements of his personality were superb. Zopyrus shocked the friends of the great Athenian sage by declaring that he saw in the contenance of Socrates the sign of strong sensuality. Socrates silenced protests with the reprimand, "Zopyrus is not mistaken; however, I have conquered those desires."

All countries have produced their quota of strong clear cool heads; and there has been rarely any lack of warm hearts. But the two are rarely combined, and the rarest phenomenon of all is a heart of mighty power working with all its force to keep the head above it cool, as a steam engine may give motion to a refrigerating machine. Such a combination occurs but once a millenium on any large scale.... The rarity of this phenomenon is due to a fundamental peculiarity of human nature. All enthusiasm, as such, tends rather to obscurity than to clearness of mental vision. The same, indeed, is the effect of emotion in general. Every emotion attracts those ideas and images which nourish it, and repels those which do not. To perceive and judge of facts with an open, unbiased mind is impossible except where impartiality, that is freedom from emotion, has first paved the way.[34]

Compare Socrates with another of the profoundest leaders of thought, Paul and Apostle, who did not possess a nature so well poised.

> For that which I do I allow not; for what I would, that do I not; but what I hate, that do I... For I know that in me (that is in my flesh) dwelleth no good thing: for the will is present with me: but how to perform that which is good I find not. For the good that I would I do not; but the evil which I would not that I do ... I find then a law that when I would do good evil is present with me. For I delight in the law of God after the inward man: But I see another law in my members, warring agaisnt the law of my mind, and bringing me into captivity to the law of sin which is in my members. O wretched man that I am! Who shall deliver me from this body of death?[35]

Third, Socrates regarded morals and practical technique or art as alike in character. A carpenter building a house, a pilot guiding his ship, a potter fashioning a vase, all alike wish to produce the best result. Their aim is simple and clear; the difficulty is merely one of means. The technique of each of these arts is resolved into the question of knowing what procedure is best fitted to produce the desired result.

Socrates regarded ethics in this same light. Every saneminded man desires to live a happy life. The goal of conduct being clear, the only problem was that of means, and that was for him an intellectual matter dependent upon insight, that is, knowledge and good judgment.

Fourth, Socrates felt that there must be a principle of unity in the virtues and in the ethical life. The Sophists denied the existence of any such universal more principle. Socrates looked for an element that was alike in all men, and he found it in *reason*. He concluded that the laws of the moral life and nature are rational and therefore true for all human beings.

What truth is there in the Socratic view? Socrates asserted that all action or conduct is determined and governed by intellectual insight. Virtue is a kind of knowledge. Ignorance is the cause of evil. He denied the state or condition which they termed "being overcome by desire." He disagreed with the Latin poet who said, "I see and approve the good but follow the bad." (*Video meliora proboque; deteriora sequor).* He believed that the intellectual life is indispensable for higher moral and ethical life.

The study of morals. To appreciate the great contribution of Socrates to the evolution of thought, it is essential to place oneself in the chaotic intellectual and moral situation of his day. Human relations had grown up through long centuries as a vast jungle of conflicting customs, habits, conventionalities, laws, restrictions, prohibitions, and taboos. These restraints were transmitted to the young by imitation, habituation, discipline, commandment, proverb, admonition, Aesopian fables, story; myth and religious symbolism. Within the various social groups, the moral customs of each had been accepted and handed on as having divine sanction. Up to this time, no one had undertaken in a scientific way to sift and study this vast morass of precept and practice.

To show the superficial and contradictory thinking that flourished, one illustration may be cited. In the *Republic*, Plato gives the following different ideas as to the nature of justice that had grown up through ages of uncritical experience:

(1) Justice is to speak the truth and to pay your debts.

(2) Justice is the interest of the stronger.

(3) Justice is to do good to friends and evil to enemies.

(4) Justice is a compromise between doing and suffering evil.

It was the self-imposed task of Socrates to subject all such thinking to a merciless examination. Out of his rigorous discussions emerged the exact nature of the virtues, their essential attributes. Thus it was that Socrates sought to reach formal definitions. The strange fact is he strove to define ethical ideas, which, of all our notions, are the least subsceptible of exactness and precision of analysis.

In all his efforts, Socrates must be credited with two great new ideas in the field of moral science. He was the first man to recognize that the intellect is an indispensable factor in any high level of ethical conduct. Again, another fact stands out in clear light: Socrates was the first man who tried to form a philosophy of the ethical life. His mind demanded a clear understanding of the nature of morals. It was his theory of ethics that led Plato to delve deeper, in order to relate the ethical nature of man to the physical and intellectual nature of the universe.

The significance of the condemnation of Socrates. Athens was by no means given to intolerance; as a matter of fact, its people were unusually friendly to novelties and innovations of all sorts. How then is the condemnation of Socrates to be explained? The indictment against him read:

Socrates is guilty because he does not acknowledge the gods which the State acknowledges, but introduces new divinities; he is guilty because he corrupts the youth.

Numerous attempts have been made to account for the voting of the death penalty against this strange figure.

To understand the situation that brought about the charges against him and the vote of condemnation, one must look at the religious and educational situation of the day, for the martyrdom of Socrates was an educational event. First, it must be recalled, Athens had been defeated by Sparta in 404 B.C. The Athenians felt that the favor of the protecting divinities of the city had been alienated, and there must be some cause for their disfavor. What better explanation need be sought than the prevailing atheism of the day? To be sure Socrates himself was an exceptionally religious man, scrupulous in worshiping the gods; but his method of teaching made men skeptical and unfaithful to the ancient divinities of the city.

The second charge explains more clearly the wrath of his fellow citizens: Socrates "corrupts the youth." His most notable disciples were notoriously lacking in the old-fashioned patriotism on which rested the defense of the city. Alcibiades, one of his most intimate followers, was a rank traitor, wholly incapable of steady loyalty to any cause. His brother, Critias, another disciple, was almost as bad, and both were bitterly hated by the Athenian democrates. Plato, too, especially in his later years, proved disloyal, advocating Spartan totalitarianism as the ideal form of government instead of the democracy of Athens. Xenophon was equally lacking in loyalty and not only became a traitor to his state but educated his three sons in Sparta. Thus the leading disciples of Socrates turned out to be lacking in those civic virtues that were most essential for the defense of Athens.

The trouble was that Socrates had sought to develop the excellences of man as a universal being rather than the qualities of the mere citizen. On the one hand, cosmopolitanism conniving with skepticism had weakened the *esprit de corps* of the Athenians and had led to their bitter defeat. On the other hand Spartan unity and training had proved its superiority over the loose and vacillating cultural training of Athens. The Athenians attributed their downfall to the education introduced by the new teachers, of whom Socrates was considered the leader. Feeling that someone must be blamed for their humiliation, they laid the responsibility upon him. There was still another cause for their hostility. Many individuals nursed a deep-seated grudge because of the biting irony of his dialectic encounters; moreover, his young followers imitated him by quizzing them to their confusion and disgust. Such, to the Athenians, were clear evidences that his influence had corrupted the youth.

The method of Socrates. The method of Socrates was as unique as his personality was striking. He did not reach conclusions, but he conducted investigations. He vehemently declined to be called wise but coined the word *philosopher*, lover of wisdom, to designate his attitude. He did not try to convey truth to students but endeavored to challenge each to think consistently and comprehensively for himself. Socrates was the symbol and representative of an age that was afire for new ideas. He yearned for clarity, understanding, insight, and general concepts as the mystic yearns for immersion in the Universal.

Before subjecting Socrates' method to critical examination, it should be stated that the florid and bombastic language and erratic notions of the sophists had succeeded only in accentuating the lack of clearness of ideas in all the higher spheres of thought at that time. Men in the highest ranks of life were incessantly wrangling about justice, self-control, and the good, without clearly and accurately discriminating the meaning of these terms. The paramount necessity for doing this was the fact that these virtues were the very ends set up by the public as the objectives of education. If these ideas were not clearly conceived, how was it possible to attain them? It was precisely this confusion of thought that made Socrates painfully aware of the need for more accurate thinking and called his genius into action. He failed, however, to see the profounder depth of knowledge to which his method ultimately led.

When Socrates in his dialogues with others professed ignorance, it was no mere artifice, nor trick of method to lure his antagonist into illogical blundering. The Socratic irony was undoubtedly due to a sincere desire to reach definite conceptions. He was by no means in the position of the modern instructor who uses the conversational method fully conscious all the time of what he wishes the student to see. Socrates was an investigator sailing unknown seas with a general idea of his goal, but without a definite chart.

Socrates did not seek to elicit answers to questions for which formal preparation of set lessons had already been made; it was not a recitation of knowledge secured second-hand, but a discussion of live issues. His method was that of reflection upon or self-criticism of the results of experience. It was a logical or dialectical examination of propositions and the testing of their truth or falsehood by their congruity or incongruity with other truth, or with experience.

Socrates wrote nothing. He even disparaged reading and writing in comparison with talking and remembering. It was his conversational method and not his results, which constitute the basis of his enduring fame. For information on his methods, two sources remain to our day: the writings of Plato, and the *Memorabilia* of Xenophon. Both of these men were followers of the celebrated sage, but each colored his account of Socrates by his individuality. Xenophon has probably given a more accurate account of the actual procedure of Socrates. One of the best examples of his method is the dialogue with Euthydemus. Socrates had heard that this talented young fellow had collected many writings and was preparing to engage in public affairs, but that he refused to receive instruction from anyone. Gradually Socrates intrigued the interest of Euthydemus, finally won his attention, and engaged him in the folflowing conversation:

Have you ever considered whether it is possible for a man who is not just to be eminent in that art? I have certainly, replied he; and it is not possible for a man to be even a good citizen without justice. Have you yourself, then, made your self master of that virtue? I think, said he, Socrates, that I shall be found not less just than any other man. Are there then works of just men, as there are works of artisans? There are, doubtless, replied he. Then, said Socrates, as artisans are able to show their works, would not just men be able also to tell their works? And why should not I, asked Euthydemus, be able to tell the works of justice; as also indeed those of injustice; for we may see and hear of no small number of them every day?

Are you willing, then, said Socrates, that we should make a delta on this side, and an alpha on that, and then we should put whatever seems to us to be a work of justice under the delta, and whatever seems to be a work of injustice under the alpha? If you think that we need those letters, said Euthydemus, make them. Socrates, having made the letters as he proposed, asked, Does falsehood then exist among mankind? It does, assuredly, replied he. Under which head shall we place it? Under injustice, certainly. Does deceit also exist? Unquestionably. Under which head shall we place that? Evidently under injustice. Does mischievousness exist? Undoubtedly and the enslaving of men? That, too, prevails. And shall neither of these things be placed by us, under justice, Euthydemus? It would be strange if they should be, said he. But, said Socrates, if a man, being chosen to lead an army, should reduce to slavery an unjust and hostile people, should we say that he committed injustice? No, certainly, replied he. Should we not rather say that he acted justly? Indisputably. And if, in the course of the war with them he sould practice deceit? That also would be just, said he. And if he should steal and carry off their property, would be not do what was just? Certainly, said Euthydemus; but I thought at first that you asked these questions only with reference to our friends. Then, said Socrates, all that we have placed under the head of injustice, we must also place under that of justice? It seems so, replied Euthydemus. Do you agree, then, continued Socrates, that having so placed them, we should make a new distinction, that it is just to do such things with regard to enemies, but unjust to do them with regard to friends, and that toward his friends our general should be as guileless as possible? By all means, replied Euthydemus. Well then, said Socrates, if a general, seeing his army dispirited, should tell them, inventing a falsehood, that auxiliaries were coming, and should by that invention check the despondency of his troops, under which head should we place such an act of deceit? It appears to me, said Euthydemus, that we must place it under justice. And if a father, when his son requires medicine and refuses to take it, should deceive him, and give him the medicine as ordinary food, and, by adopting such deception should restore him to health, under which head must we place such an act of deceit? It appears to me that we must put it under the same head. And if a person, when his friend was in despondency, should, through fear that he might kill himself, steal or take away his sword, or any other weapon, under which head must we place that act? That, assuredly, we must place under justice. You say, then, said Socrates, that not even toward our friends must we act on all occasions without deceit? We must not indeed, said he, for I retract what I said before, if I may be permitted to do so. It is indeed much better that you should be permitted, said Socrates, than that you should not place actions on the right side. But of those who deceive their friends in order not to injure them (that we may not leave even this point unconsidered), which of the two is the more unjust: he who does so intentionally or he who does so involuntarily? Indeed, Socrates, said Euthydemus, I no longer put confidence in the answer which I give; for all that I said before appears to me now to be quite different from what I then thought; however, let me venture to say that he who deceives intentionally is more unjust than he who deceives involuntarily.

There then followed discussion as to what things are good, with the same result. Then Socrates attacked the question of democracy and Euthydemus became utterly confused.

> He went away accordingly, in great dejection, holding himself in contempt, and thinking that he was in reality no better than a slave.

Of those who were thus addressed by Socrates, many came to him no more; and these be regarded as too dull to be improved. But Euthydemus, on the contrary, conceived that he could by no other means become an estimable character than by associating with Socrates as much as possible; and he is consequence never quitted him, unless some necessary business obliged him to do so. He also imitated many of his habits.

When Socrates saw that he was thus disposed, he no longer puzzled him with questions, but explained to him, in the simplest and clearest manner, what he thought that he ought to know, and what it would be best for him to study.[36]

The Beginnings of Educational Theory

The educational problem became central. It is customary for scholars, historians, and writers on the history of philosophy to approach this era from their respective points of view. This narrowness leads to misinterpretation and distorted emphasis. The central principle, the motivating idea in the later Periclean Age was educational. This was true for dramatists, philosophers, and statesmen. The sophists were teachers primarily and only secondarily investigators of ethical concepts, literary critics, or philosophers. Socrates, as he himself claimed, was an educator of youth, not a professional philosopher. Plato was an educational thinker first, but in order to solve the educational problem as he saw it, he was obliged to become metaphysician, political economist, psychologist, and ethical thinker. The educational point of view sets the confusion of this era into rational order.

The Periclean revolution produced the need for a more elaborate knowledge and a more efficient technique in every walk of life. This need emerged so suddenly that the old education failed to prepare the youth for the new conditions. The days of simplicity in the industrial arts and in the concerns of war and the state were gone. Rank amateurs, however intelligent, could no longer perform these services efficiently. The day of expert practitioners and specialized workers had come. The chief trouble arose from the complete lack of any agencies to train young men in the technique of generalship, statecraft, domestic economy, and political leadership. Athens had become a pure democracy and, as a democracy, had to have leaders who were equipped not only to formulate new policies, but to persuade the people to adopt some course of action. For example, a general not only had to lead the army efficiently, but he had first to persuade the people that his plan of campaign would prove to be the most advantageous one.

New educational problems. Out of the socio-political conditions emerged a number of pressing educational problems which challenged the deepest thinking of the best citizens of Athen. There were five of these problems:

(1) Is virtue, or, to use a more modern term, is civic efficiency teachable? This is equivalent to the question: Can good citizens be formed by instruction? The discussion of this question raised the deeper problem of the nature of virtue itself. Is it the gift of the gods? The result of heredity—or of habit? Does it come from instruction? Events had made the Greeks conscious that intelligence is an actual force in the world. It produces order and control. The problem arose as to the relation of intelligence to virtue. If the good are happy, does intelligence help us to be good? This profound inquiry formed the central problem of all Greek thought from the fifth century onward. The sophist declared virtue teachable. Socrates maintained that intelligence is a pre-requisite to goodness of all kinds. Plato decided that the higher virtues depend upon instruction because they are due to intelligence. Xenophon, on the contrary, thought intellectual instruction unimportant. Isocrates did not believe justice and wisdom could be transmitted by instruction, and neither did Aristotle.

(2) The question next in importance was whether education is a family or a state function. On this problem, the Greek world became sharply divided. In the early days every Greek state was an organism in which the citizen lived and had his whole being; he never felt any antagonism between his own interest and that of the state. There was complete subordination of the individual will to the will of the community. Sparta was the most perfect embodiment of

this totalitarian policy. Athens, on the contrary, favored tribal and family life. The decisive victory of Spartan arms over the Athenians signalized the superiority of the Spartan type of government and training over the Athenian. Pericles had boasted "We live at ease. Our military training is in many respects superior to that of our adversaries." He pitted the democracy of Athens with its system of private education against the totalitarian policy of Sparta with its rigorous system of regimentation. Athens lost.

The inevitable conclusion was that virtue or civic efficiency is an affair of the state and can be inculcated only by a public system of education. Private or family education does not promote state *esprit de corps*.

Because of these experiences, the question of the relation of the state to education became a major issue for the first time in the history of institutional life. Plato and Xenophon became ardent advocates of state education. Aristotle followed in their footsteps. Isocrates believed in the control of the Areopagus over education, but he substituted the panhellenic ethos for the city state as the object of patriotic devotion.

(3) With the new need for a more adequate general education than the youth received in the elementary music school, this problem arose: What should constitute the curriculum of this secondary education? Should it be general or specialized? The sophists believed the natural sciences and language arts were the best preparation for higher studies. Isocrates, the leading educator of this period, thought rhetoric was the best subject. Plato, as an idealist and believer in formal discipline, advocated mathematics, astronomy, and harmony.

(4) In the field of higher instruction there was a sharp division of opinion. Some believed in philosophy; others in rhetoric and oratory; some in military training. Which should it be?

(5) What should be the new educational ideal or objective? Here again great diversity of opinion arose. Plato believed the ideal life must be spent in the pursuit of the true, the beautiful, and the good, and consequently he favored the ideal of the scholar who devotes his time to knowledge. Aristotle agreed that the scholar's life is happy, but it is not the best. Numerous substitutes were offered in place of civic patriotism as the center of character cultivation. Xenophon advocated the Spartan system; Isocrates urged loyalty to panhellenic culture. The Stoics introduced the religion of rationalism and a life of self-control; the Epicureans advocated personal pleasure, but it must be self-indulgence with discretion. Each of these had its votaries; but no one of them became dominant. The situation is well summarized by Jebb as follows:

> In the normal Greek conception society and the state were one. The man had no existence apart from the citizen; morality was inseparable from civic virtue. But meanwhile new intellectual and moral needs had come into being to which the limited elasticity of the state-life could no longer respond; and on the other hand Greek democracy had passed the point up to which, organized as it was, it was capable of a healthy growth. The individual had begun to draw more and more away from the state. Instead of the citizen's duty being the standard of spiritual life, the needs of individual development became the measure of what could reasonable be expected from the citizen. The most striking proof of this is the decay, almost disappearance, of a virtue which had its roots in the idea of the state—readiness for personal selfsacrifice. Active love of one's own city—the central instinct of healthy Greek life—begins to merge in contemplative citizenship of the world.[37]

The new era produced much discussion of these educational problems. Only four of the great theorists on education can be discussed here, the reactionary Xenophon, the chief teacher Isocrates, and then at greater length, Plato and Aristotle.

XENOPHON (430-355 B.C.)

Xenophon was primarily a soldier of fortune and a journalist, very fastidious about dress and deportment. He possessed but shallow intellectual gifts; and although he displayed a certain many-sidedness of character, he never rose above the mediocre. His greatest work was the *Memorabilia* in which he portrays the teaching of Socrates. He was not a good biographer, however, for his vanity warped and distorted all his perceptions, and his lack of insight rendered his work superficial.

Xenophon lacked patriotism. He fought against his native city and was banished for treason. During the greater part of his life he lived in exile. If all these things are true, why spend time studying his ideas? Because he may be taken as a type of many in Athens who at the time were dismayed at the trend in events, and who proposed to remedy the troubles by a changed system of education. He is a thoroughgoing reactionary, a conservative who harks back to the "good old days," and the old training. In his *Oeconomicus* he pictured the education of women; in the *Cyropaedia* the education of boys and young men; in the *Memorabilia* he described the instruction of Socrates.

Doctrine of the state. As a young man, Xenophon was a follower of Socrates, but after reaching manhood he spent scarcely any time in his native city. He was totally averse to the democratic institutions and training of the Athenians. Spartan training was for him the ideal form of education and government. Most of his life was passed in company of Spartan soldiers on foreign campaigns, and when he settled down, he made his home close to Sparta.

The fact of the matter was that Xenophon lacked the intelligence necessary for comprehending the intellectual revolution of the time. Like all conservatives who have little discernment, he was wanting in clear insight into sociological phenomena. With Aristophanes and others he attached the blame for existing conditions to the new education, which was at that very moment laboring heroically to bring a new era to birth. The actual cause of the bad social and political conditions lay mainly in the weakness of the old education itself. This same education, they now proposed to restore as a remedy.

In casting about for a new and more satisfactory view, Xenophon was attracted by Sparta. She was at the head of the Greek civilization so far as military power was concerned. What was more natural than to consider her rigorous system of education the cause. It was in complete accord with his reactionary tendencies, and his military and sporting inclinations. Accordingly, in place of the loose system of private education which appeared to be flat failure, he decided in favor of a strict military system supported and controlled by the state.

In the *Cyropaedia* Xenophon set forth his scheme of education. His fundamental principle was that education is the business of the state; it is not for the sake of the individual, but solely for the common good. The city square contains the government buildings which are divided into four parts. One part belongs to the boys, one to young men, the third to the men of mature years, and the last to the old men who are past the age of military service. All are required to report to their quarters every day; the youth guard the buildings at night. Over each of these groups there are twelve officers, one from each tribe of the city. Those who preside over the boys and over the youth are selected because of their educational ability. The education of the boys is alongthe line of self-government. Xenophon stated that they go to school to learn justice, just as in other places they go to learn to read and write. A sense of gratitude, self-control, obedience to officers, temperance, courage and endurance were the virtues sought.

Young men of sixteen or seventeen are to be trained for military service. For ten years they act as a guard to the government buildings. They are to be taken on hunting expeditions as a preparation for war. Most of the time is to be spent in acquiring skill in the use of arms, and in military evolutions. In this plan is contained the idea for the ephebic college that some years later was established in Athens.

In his scheme of education, Xenophon omitted all reference to letters. Though a prolific writer himself, he did not provide the youth with literary training. How far he stood from his master Socrates! How slightly he appreciated the intellectual progress of the day! We do not hear a word of the Socratic doctrine of identity of knowledge and virtue. Further, he rejected music in the narrow sense.

Education of women. The attitude of Xenophon toward womanhood and the education of girls may be gathered from the conversation of Socrates, to which reference has already been made.[38] We can easily understand the viewpoint of Xenophon from the pious, commonplace reason which he assigns for the sphere of woman's life and education. "Endeavor by all means," Ischomachus tells his wife, "to do in the best possible manner those duties which the gods have qualified you to do, and which custom approved." When men of ordinary ability wish to defend the present order, they usually ascribe it to divine sanction. The gods have made woman weaker than man; therefore she should give herself exclusively to household duties. The ordering of the house, the care of the younger children, instruction of the servants—such are the limits of woman's work and of her education. Xenophon rejected every other feature of Athenian education except that of their narrow training of women; in this he adhered to Athenian custom.

ISOCRATES (436-338 B.C.)

Isocrates was the most successful professional teacher of antiquity, and one of the few who had a definite theory of education. He was born in Athens. His father was wealthy and provided him the best training obtainable. As a young man he was a favorite of Socrates, who prophesied his greatness; but he also received instruction from several of the leading sophists.

Isocrates did not engage in political activity as might naturally be expected of one so gifted. He frankly confessed the reason: "Nature denied me force for action, and gave me but imperfect talents for speech."[39] Though he was the most illustrious rhetorician of the day, his weak voice precluded a career on the public platform. Having lost his fortune, he set up a school near the Lyceum in 492 B.C. There he taught rhetoric and wrote political pamphlets until his death at the age of ninety-eight.

His school was the most celebrated in antiquity. Students flocked to him from all parts of the world. He counted among them statesmen, generals, and even kings. Cicero declared that the eloquence of all Greece "was trained and perfected" under his instruction. His students became the most brilliant orators, advocates, statesmen, philosophers, historians, and teachers of rhetoric. In 351 B.C. a contest of eloquence, open to all Greece, was held at Halicarnassos in which every competitor who presented himself had been a pupil of Isocrates. So celebrated was his school that a book was compiled with the title *The Disciples of Isocrates.*

Theory and practice of education. Isocrates was more than a skillful technician. He had a clear view of what to aim at, and he chose with precision the means to attain this end. Two principles were emphasized in his theory and practice of education.

(1) The first principle was this: the power of oratory does not rest on mere rules or technicalities of rhetoric. He despised as deeply as Plato the rogues who employed the subtleties of rhetoric merely to win an argument or persuade a jury. Public speech, he contended, must find its power in rational ideas and knowledge. When speaking of the Athenians he evaluated the old education and its results in the most laudatory terms.

> They were characterized in all things by the unselfish spirit. They were thrifty of the resources of the state; they were sensitively loyal to its honour and to its interest in their

> personal conduct and in their legislation. Political parties, political clubs, they vied only in benefits to the city. Thus were formed the men who, surpassing the captors of Troy, vanquished Asia; men whose merit transcends all that has been said or sung of them.[40]

But while the old education had performed admirable service, he was aware that this knowledge was necessary for the accomplishment of life's ends.

(2) The second principle of Isocrates was that education must be practical in the higher sense of the term. Oratory was not a mere embellishment, but a precision instrument for practical use in the larger political affairs of the civilized world. His curriculum was broad, but, like his master, Socrates, he had no concern for knowledge for its own sake. He stated his position as follows:

> Geometry, astrology, eristic dialogues are good for the young, if only as employing them; but they do not make practical men. By an educated man I understand one who can deal with all that comes upon him day by day: who is honest and mannerly in society; who rules his desires; who is not spoiled by good fortune.[41]

(3) Isocrates was more than a technical rhetorician; he was a practical idealist who desired to raise rhetoric and oratory to a genuine art. He held as much in contempt those teachers who claimed too much for their instruction as he did those who used oratory for low purposes.

> He held that not only may prose be artistic but that the utterance of rhetoric may be, ought to be, a work of art as complete and as substantive as the utterance of poetry; that it has its own ascertainable laws of rhythm and of harmony; and that the artist who having mastered these laws, addressed himself to the treatment of a great subject, had with him a power, beside and beyond the strength of his cause or of his genius—a power coming to him, as to the poet, through his art, and springing from an essential music latent in language which his art has shown him how to bring upon his ear.[42]

We see from this statement that the best of the teachers of rhetoric was fully aware of the value of combining art with the useful. He knew that Greek oratory by its use of rhythm produced subtle effects—which elude the duller sensibilities of modern speakers and audiences.

(4) The great objective of Isocrates was Hellenic unity. All the resources of knowledge and of the rhetorical art were to be employed in this noble cause. This unity was to be a spiritual or cultural order and not merely one of blood. He emphatically stated,

> A man is not considered in the fullest sense a Hellene merely because he is of Hellenic blood, unless, further, he bears the stamp of the Athenian mind.[43]

Isocrates possessed a passionate admiration for his native Athens and for the culture of all the Greeks. He devoted his talent through his long life to the unification of the Greek world against barbarian influences. His ideal of the educated man was one who mastered the art of rhetoric in order to spread liberty and Hellenic culture throughout the world.

Weakness of moral training in old Athens. The older Athenians did not rely on laws to make good citizens, for they clearly understood the true relation of citizenship to character. They realized that civic virtues are not due to mere instruction or to information. For the cultivation of character they relied upon family discipline, respect for their elders, supervision by the court of the Areopagus, *esprit de corps,* and devotion to the common welfare. When these influences ceased to function, individual interests multiplied, and patriotism declined.

In spite of many excellences in the old education, moral conditions in Athens and all over Greece degenerated. The sea was infested with pirates, the land by marauders. Traitors were admired for their cleverness. The citizens, once the first to fight for the city, remained at home—while the army was recruited from foreign mercenaries. Fighting became a profession, but the spirit of sacrifice for the public welfare was dead. The people were content to sponge on the bounty of the state.

Having forsaken their civic ideals, which were their real deities, their strength was sapped, and the Greeks lost their political independence to peoples no more vigorous and even less intelligent than themselves, but possessing a stronger spirit of unity. Individualism, treason, and love of ease, destroyed the city-states. It is a familiar fact to students of human progress that the spirit of man cannot find permanent satisfaction in any small and unchangeable organization. Thought and action perpetually expand and, as a consequence, demand an environment commensurate with their larger grasp in which to function. Isocrates, Plato, and the Stoic, each in his own way, saw the necessity of a more comprehensive organization of mankind. Alexander the Great made the first attempt to universalize the Hellenic spirit and the humanistic culture which it produced. But the Greek was never sufficiently broad in his sympathies or in understanding human relations to evolve the larger unity that could stabilize life. Thus Greek civilization went down because there was no inner principle, no commanding ethos of thought and feeling. This failure offers a clear warning that the human spirit is universal in its scope and must have a social ideal commensurate with its inner potentialities.

NOTES

1. Dickinson, G. Lowes. *The Greek View of Life*, pp. 115-116. New York: Doubleday, Page & Co., 1927.

2. Because of this praise of a rival city. Pindar was fined by his home town. The Athenians, however, gave him twice the amount of the fine and set up a bronze statue in his honour.

3. Gomperz, Theodore, *Greek Thiners*, Vol. I, pp. 382-383.

4. Livingstone, R.W., *The Greek Genius and Its Meaning to Us*, Second Edition, p. 206. Oxford: Clarendon Press, 1915.

5. Pragmatic philosophy loudly deplores the separation of culture and the pursuit of science from practical affairs. This philosophy is based upon the theory that thought or ideas evolve in connection with particular practical problems or situations. It assumes that empirical practice is the only condition under which thought has evolved. It must be recognized, however, that it was the divorce of thought from practical affairs that produced the evolution of higher thinking and also of art in fifth century Greece. The leisure afforded the higher classes was one of the conditions of that higher development of intelligence. At any rate the separation of thought and practical life which Dr. John Dewey *(Democracy and Education,* Chapter XIX. New York: the Macmillan Co., 1924) and his school so greatly bewail marked this period. Moreover, the fact remains that none of the great civilizations in which empirical practice dominated thought and action produced the highest level of mentality. Only the Greeks who got away from the practical activities of life make this important ascent. As Aristotle points out they wanted to know not "on account of any utility" but for "the sake of understanding."

6. Livingstone, *op. cit.*, p. 208.

7. Livingstone, R.W., *op. cit.*, p. 208.

8. Chapman, John Jay, *Lucian, Plato and Greek Morals*, pp. 25-56. Boston: Houghton Miffin Company, 1931.

9. Rawlinson, George, *Herodotus*, Vol. II, p. 363.

10. Fairbanks, Arthur, *op. cit.*, p. 266.

11. *Ibid.*, pp. 266-267.

12. Gulick, C.B., *Athenaeus: The Deipnosophists.* Vol. IV, p. 373. Cambridge: Loeb Classical Library, 1930. By permission of the President and Fellows of Harvard College.

13. Roggers, B.B., Aristophanes, *Frogs,* Vol. II, 11. 1066—67. Cambridge: Leob Classical Library: 1924.

14. *Ibid.*, Vol. II, 11. 1096-70.

15. See page 243 of this text.

16. Dakyns, H.G., (Tr.) *The Works of Xenophon*, Vol. III, p. 95, London: Macmillan and Company, 1897.

17. Dakyns, H.G., *op. cit.*, p. 279 Dakyns ascribes this work to Xenophon, but others dispute his conclusion.

18. Plato, *Protagoras*, § 310.

19. *Ibid.*, *Meno*, §§ 11-12.

20. Rogers, Benjamin Bickley, *Aristophanes, The Clouds*, Vol. I, p. 355, Cambridge: Loeb Classical Library, 1924.

21. Farrell, George S. *Greek Luric Poetry*, pp. 40-41. London: Longmans, Green & Co., 1891.

22. Livingstone, R.W., *The Greek Genius and Its Meaning to Us*, p. 177, Second Edition. Oxford: Clarendon Press, 1915.

23. Livingstone, Richard Winn, *op. cit.*, p. 209.

24. Before this, individual philosophers had associated young men with themselves and taught their systems of thought. Pythagoras formed a monastic institution with a definite regimen. The association of these men was for the purpose of propaganda and the practice of a certain way of life.

25. Plato, *Protagoras*, § 318.

26. See Hicks, R.D., *Diogenes Laertius, Lives of Eminent Philosophers*, Vol. II, pp. 463-467. Cambridge: Leob Classical Library, 1925.

27. For this tale, see Xenophon. *Memorabilia*, Book II, Chapter 1.

28. Grote, George, *A History of Greece*, Chapter LXVII.

29. *Encyclopaedia Britannica*, Article. "Sophists," 11th Edition.

30. Plato, *Symposium*, § 220. For Socrates' life and character read Gomperz, *Greek Thinkers*, Vol. II; for his death read Plato's *Apology* and *Crito;* for his method read the *Memorabilia* of Xenophon.

31. At various times when he was about to enter upon some activity, an inner voice spoke to him and warned him against the action. This monitor he took to be a divine providence and trusted to it implicity. It marked him as different though he never presumed overmuch on account of this remarkable peculiarity.

32. Dakyns, H.G., *The Works of Xenophon*, Vol. III, p. 5. London: Macmillan and Company, 1897.

33. Plato, *Protagoras*, § 182.

34. Gomperz, Theodore, *Greek Thinkers*, Vol. II, p. 48.

35. *Episile to the Romans*, 7: 15-24.

36. Xenophon, *The Memorabilia of Socrates*, translated by Rev. J.S. Watson. New York: Arthur Hinds & Co.

37. Jebb, R.C., *The Attic Orators*, Vol. II, pp. 15-16. London: Macmillan and Company, 1876.

38. Jebb, R.C., *op. cit,*, Vol. II, p. 115.

39. Jebb, R.C., *op. cit.*, Vol. II, p. 155.

40. Jebb, R.C., *op. cit.*, Vol. II, p. 115.

41. Jebb, R.C., *op. cit.*, Vol. II, pp. 55-56.

42. Jebb, *op. cit.*, Vol. II, p. 154.

3

Education during Ninth to Twelfth Centuries

"Education makes a people easy to lead,
but difficult to drive; easy to govern,
but impossible to enslave."

—**Lord Brougham**

"The Things taught in schools and colleges are not an education, but the means of education."

—**Emerson**

To be obsessed with the idea that education and schools are synonymous is a handicap in studying any period of the history of education; but it makes simply impossible an intelligent evaluation of education in the 'Dark Ages.' It is that obsession which has misled many historians to exaggerate the value of Charlemagne's influence upon the education of the period, and even to trace a connection between his efforts on behalf of schools and the marked intellectual revival which took place in Europe in the twelfth and thirteenth centuries, three or four hundred years after the death of Charlemagne. There is a manifest huge gap to be bridged between these two ages; and it is not bridged by schools.[1] This chapter will try to show how the barbarian Europe of the ninth century came to be the civilized Europe of the thirteenth century; the process is essentially one of education.

'Dark Ages' Continue After Charlemagne

It is no injustice to Charlemagne's fine efforts to say

that they had little to do with bringing light to the 'Dark Ages.' If the vigorous government of Charlemagne had been maintained with equal vigour by his successors, and if these successors had shown the same wise interest in education which was one of the chief glories of Charlemagne, a scant hundred years might have put an end to the 'Dark Ages.' But the statement is painfully like the old saying in the army, "If we had some ham, we could have ham and eggs, if we only had some eggs." Charlemagne's efforts on behalf of schools practically died with him. His successors were, for the most part, incompetent to further them. More than that, important as those efforts were, they were limited even in his own time. They had not a wide enough influence to affect the general state of education in Europe. The Germanies were scarcely touched by them. Spain was almost wholly in the power of the Saracens. The Christian East, struggling desperately against the Moslems, was in disorder; it was only in 860, half a century after the death of Charlemagne, that Michael III was able to refound the University of Constantinople; and the restoration was not very vigorous even then.[2] In Charlemagne's own domain, the schools he set up would have needed generations to make an impression upon the feudal anarchy of the times.

Early Feudalism Anarchic

We must not let the military successes and glory of Charlemagne blind us to the fact that Europe was still seething in barbarian ferment. The civilization of the Middle Ages was still in its feeble infancy. The most important organization of society was in local efforts to climb out of anarchy. Small freeholders banded together for mutual aid, their immediate aim being merely security of life and property. It was an organization primarily for war, not for the development of civilization. It was a most necessary organization; but its very necessity is a terrible revelation of the bad conditions which prevailed. Out of it some fine things were to grow; but they were not envisaged in the early organization itself. It affected but very little the wretched slavery which the various peoples of Europe had inherited from the Romans or had brought from their own vague antiquity. Feudalism of itself did nothing to improve the lot of the slaves and serfs; it merely included them in the compacts which their masters made. Later, as we shall see, it tended indirectly to give to the serf a slightly better status, by attaching him to the land. He was no longer to be a mere chattel; he had some roots in the soil. But the whole of society, despite its elaborate organization in detail, was so loosely knit together as scarcely to merit the name of a society. This exaggerated local independence was a great hindrance to the spread of any general scheme of education, such as Charlemagne had hoped and striven for. Even in 885, seventy years after the death of Charlemagne, a like attempt of Alfred in England came to practically nothing, and for precisely the same reasons.[3]

The Church Involved in Feudalism

It is to be noted that all of Charlemagne's zeal for schools found its practical expression through the clergy and the monks. Not even the most hostile writer disputes the fact that these churchmen were in almost exclusive possession of what educational tools the age could look to.[4] Charlemagne had no choice but to use the clergy and the monks. And it must be frankly admitted that most of them were poor instruments. One Alcuin does not make a learned and pious clergy, any more than one swallow makes a summer. The bishops and the abbots had become feudal lords; no doubt, by sheer necessity. But the fact involved them, and through them the priests and monks, in the turbulent anarchy of the time, in the riot of individualism, which, sifting all elements, we find at the bottom of barbarism. For all practical purposes each bishopric, each abbey, stood by itself; concerned chiefly, if not only, with its relations to its feudal suzerains and feudal subjects. Bishops and abbots were more interested in caring for their feudal rights than in raising the tone of civilization, either morally or intellectually.

Conditions Made Worse by Further Barbarian Raids

Baronius is perhaps the first to give to the ninth and tenth centuries the name of the 'Iron Age.' It was an age marked not merely by constant feudal quarrels, but by savage and destructive inroads from the still less civilized outer world. There are three of these invasions to be specially noted. The first is the Norman raids, which occupied the greater part of the ninth century, and ended only in the shameless bribe by which Charles the Simple, in 911, turned over to the pirate Rollo the splendid Duchy of Normandy. Then, beginning in 831, the Saracens ravaged northern Italy and southern France, pushing up the valley of the Rhone. More terrible still, huge armies of Huns devastated central Europe during most of the tenth century. In 926 their savage waves had come up to the very frontiers of Lorraine; and they continued in a succession of invasions until the death of their leader Tatsong in 972.

With Particularly Disastrous Results to Clergy and Monks

Such events alone would demoralize even a well-established civilization; they were incredibly injurious to the difficult beginnings of mediaeval civilization. All the elements of society suffered through the confusion and insecurity brought about by these invasions, but perhaps the clergy and the monks suffered most of all. Their material losses were great. The Norman pirate, Hastings, in 851, burned the monasteries of Fontanelles, St. Ouen, and Jumieges. Within a few years, Marmoutier was pillaged, St. Martin of Tours was burned, Malmedy, Corbie, Liege, and scores of others, were destroyed. In the course of the ninth century, the abbey of Nonantula in Italy was plundered seven times, ending with the last savage onslaught of the Huns, who in 899 killed all the monks together with their abbot, Gregory. It has been said that by the beginning of the tenth century scarcely one of the great French abbeys was left standing. Many of these monasteries had possessed considerable libraries. Fontanelles had a famous one. The chronicles of Novalesa in Italy record that when the Saracen invaders came, in 906, the fleeing monks carried away with them to Turin more than six thousand volumes. Most of these were later burned by the Sarcens in the sack of Turin. Beyond a doubt the monastery libraries suffered great losses in all these raids and invasions. But more grievous to mediaeval society was the demoralization of the monks and clergy, caused by their dispersion and the inevitable breakdown of what religious discipline the rude times had been able to boast. Wars always tend to breed license.[5]

The Darkest Part of the 'Dark Ages'

Shephards and sailors and other watchers of the night have made us believe that the darkest hours come before the dawn. Certainly, the latter part of the 'Dark Ages' grows steadily more gloomy. Rulers were incompetent; and what energies they had were almost entirely dovoted to war. There was no cohesion in the social order, little or no intercommunication of ideas. Roads had pretty nearly ceased to exist.[6] All life was narrowed to the small circle of feudal domains; and even that life was made sullen and savage by its insecurity. The Catholic Church, the one great hope of civilization in these turbulent times, found only pitifully feeble instruments to its hand, in a dispersed and demoralized huddle of monks, in its swaggering, incontinent, and ignorant bishops and priests.[7] Perhaps in no part of Europe were conditions worse than in Rome itself, during most of this time torn by factions which made the papacy the sport of their ambitions.

Optimistic writers try to see an area of light amidst all this darkness, in the Germany of the Ottos. But the exception there is more apparent than real. In the tenth century, the descendants of Henry the Fowler, and notably Otto the Great, who ruled as king from 936 to 973, and was crowned emperor of the West by the Pope at Rome in 962, established a strongly autocratic government in Germany, and made a vigorous stand against the Hun invaders. But far from curbing the turbulence of the age, they added to it by engaging in the fractional wars of Italy. Otto the Great appointed his brother, St. Bruno, and his cousins, Poppo and Henry, to episcopal sees. These were three good men, who tried earnestly to stir up some enthusiasm for learning and piety amongst their clergy. But the little good they did was more than offset by the vicious policy which gave them their appointment as bishops, and which led to such grave abuses in the Church. And they no more succeeded in making a home for learning in Germany, or in effecting any widespread reform in the German clergy or people, than had Charlemagne in France or Alfred in England.

Needed Revival

What the age needed was, not a scattering of learned men, not an occasional pious bishop here and there, not even a wise sovereign who would encourage schools. If the education of men was to develop in any way befitting human beings, society needed two things. The first was a definite stabilizing, on some sound and healthy basis, suited in a practical way to what the men of the time were capable of appreciating. And the second was a moral reform, some return to Christian principles of conduct. These two processes would constitute the real education of Europe, and upon them alone could be built any further development of civilization. The instruments of these two processes were at hand; in the tradition of Roman law and the civil organization, which, though obscured, had never been wholly lost to Europe; and in the Catholic Faith, which smouldered with a divine vitality under all the ashes of violence, simony, ignorance, superstition, and immorality. But that Europe of the ninth and tenth centuries should be so revivified would seem to be a greater moral miracle than even the survival of the Church during the first three centuries of persecution.

Brought about through Cluny

It is no exaggeration to say that the foundation of

Cluny marks the turning point in the history of education in the Middle Ages. Cluny was a Benedictine abbey, about four miles from Macon, founded in 910 by Berno, on a grant of land from William, the Duke of Aquitaine. There had been Benedictine monasteries continiously for nearly four hundred years. In their early history, as we have seen, the Benedictine monks were a most important factor in the civilizing of the barbarians. But although all the monasteries had a common 'rule,' or way of life, each monastery was an isolated unit. That fact involved them in the feudal organization which grew up round about them. Further, it exposed them to the great weakness of being unable to resist or oppose the bad conditions which might prevail in their particular locality; they had no common fund of spiritual vigor upon which to draw in their need. Hence they inevitably suffered decay in the social anarchy of the ninth century. Berno saw the need of closer organization, for the mutual support of the monasteries. During the seventeen years of his government of the new abbey of Cluny, he succeeded in getting five other monasteries to revive the spirit of the old Benedictine rule,[8] and to place themselves under the central jurisdiction of Cluny. His successor, St. Odo, abbot from 927 to 942, added seventeen more abbeys to the organization. Both Odo and Maieul, who was abbot from 948 to 975, carried the new spirit into Italy, which had perhaps suffered more greviously from the distress of the times than any other country. Bishop Gennadius of Astorga, in Spain, restored a number of abbeys destroyed by the Saracens, and placed them under the rule of Cluny.[9] And so the organization grew, until, in the twelfth century, three hundred and fourteen Benedictine houses were included in the Cluny system.[10] It was this growing system which changed the character of feudalism, and therefore of all mediaeval society. The change was an amazing work of education.

Which Brought Back the Roman Concept of Organization

As has been said, early feudal society needed stabilizing.

All its elements were in flux. A great man like Charlemagne could hold them together momentarily with his strong hand; but when his grasp was relaxed, they scattered again. Yet the memory of the great Roman organization was never wholly lost, even during the wildest times of anarchy in Europe. Indeed, from the time of Charlemagne on, there were repeated efforts to revive the Roman Empire itself. For the most part the revivals were in name only. When they approached any reality, it was always by a mere forced imposition of physical power: a necessarily unstable condition. Now the reform of Cluny was modeled on the Roman idea of a central organization; but it did not impose that central government; it got men to accept it voluntarily.[11] It is true, Cluny was concerned with organizing a comparatively small number of men, in the distintive (and what some would stupidly call 'unsocial') monastic life. But those monks were an influential part of mediaeval society, and their monasteries were intricately involved in the feudal system. The drawing together of the monks could not but affect the complicated feudal world in which they lived. A new idea of union was actively at work in that world, and its value appealed to many, who had no notion whatever that it was a very old idea brought again into practice.[12] It would be out of proportion, and beyond our purpose, to follow the development of that idea in the feudal system. Every honest history of the Middle Ages shows it. But we should not forget that it takes its beginning at Cluny.

And Revived the Christian Spirit

More important even than the civil reform of feudalism, was the revival of Christian principles of living; without which, indeed, the civil reform itself would have been impossible. It must not be forgotten that by the tenth century most of western Europe had accepted Christianity in theory at least; but it is always a harder task to get people to reduce a theory to practice than to get them to accept the theory. Even those who may not admit that moral and religious education is more important than intellectual education,[13] must confess that it is more difficult. Cluny set about the moral education of Europe both by example and by precept. Within fifty years of its foundation, the holy lives of its own monks had made the name of Cluny famous throughtout the Western world, had impressed the imagination of peasants and nobles alike, and had begun to leave the mass of Europe.

Immediately by its Influence on the Clergy and Monks

The Popes John XI and Leo VII welcomed and furthered this revival. By their charters they exempted Cluny from all jurisdiction save their own. They made of the Cluniacs a rock in the swirling waters of feudalism. Bishops turned to Cluny for aid in reforming various monasteries; often to find the peaceful Cluniacs ending by reforming the bishop himself. It is impossible to reckon accurately the number of restorations and new foundations of monasteries in the tenth century, but in the lifetime of Odo alone we have record of more than fifty in France, Italy, and the Germanies. The Christian fervor of the monks was contagious. Often, as in Upper Lorraine, laymen and the lower clergy besieged the bishops with clamors for reform; this was very notable in Toul, Verdun, and Metz. Corruptio optimi pessima: a bad bishop is harder to Christianize than a prostitute; but at times even a bad bishop gave way to popular demand, as Adalbero did at Metz in 933.[14] It is not implied that suddenly all the clergy and monks became saints; but unquestionably the moral and religious tone of the clergy and monks was raised, the scandal of dissolute clerical lives was lessened, the teachings of Christ were more earnestly preached to the people at large. There are three particular effects of this educational movement to be noted.

By Introducing the Truce of God

First, and perhaps most important, was the repression of feudal violence. In 989, at the Council of Charroux,[15] was decreed the Pax Dei; by which the sentence of excommunication was uttered against all who should attack unarmed travellers, steal from a church, or steal from the poor. It was declared again at Narbonne and at Le Puy, in 990; more solemnly at Poitiers, in 999.[16] Twenty like councils repeated the decree between 1000 and 1038. This was a significant stand against the anarchic violence of feudalism; and it is to be observed that it is distinctly based on religious belief and backed by religious sanction. But it was to go further. At the Council of Elne, in 1027, the 'truce of God' was first proposed: an agreement by which the knights bound themselves not to fight "from the ninth hour on Saturday to the first hour of Monday."[17] Within fifteen years the movement had grown so that Odilo, the fifth abbot of Cluny, backed by Reginald, the Archbishop of Arles, Benedict, the Bishop of Avignon, and Nithard, the Bishop of Nice, could appeal to the clergy of Italy to receive and keep the Treva Dei, "which we have accepted and firmly hold."[18] This developed truce of God was to extent from sunset on Wednesday to sunrise on Monday. The days of peace between Wednesday and Monday were to be kept sacred to the memory of the Christian mysteries; the motive of peace was the Christian religion. For a homicide committed on a day of the Truce, the penalty was exile from the province and pilgrimage to Jerusalem; for other offenses against the peace, reparation under the civil law, and a double canonical penance. It is astounding to know that the truce of God was accepted; even though it was not perfectly kept, its acceptance marked a great educational advance; and it was kept in sufficient measure to lift Europe out of anarchy.[19]

By Christianizing the Institution of Chivalry

Chivalry at first meant only cavalry, soldiers on horseback. Later it meant the order of feudal nobility, based upon the military and social distinction of knighthood. In theory, knighthood was not hereditary. It was to be conferred as a recognition of valor and worthiness. It was to be a democratic institution, open to every one who could earn entry into it. In reality, of course, it was practically hereditary; with rare exceptions, only the sons of knights became knights. For centuries the distinction of knighthood was nothing more than a distinction of physical prowess; and if to our modern minds the very name is filled with the fine moral flavor of loyalty, devoted courage, courtesy, if today chivalrous means considerate, unselfish, and morally noble, we must recall that the change in meaning came from that Cluny which introduced the truce of God. The Chansons de Geste read back into the earlier chivalry a spirit which it did not have until the influence of the Cluniac monks made Christian principles an essential part of chivalry. Without ceasing to be military, chivalry became religious.[20] Its ceremonies of initation were acts of worship of God. The oath of knighthood was an oath to defend religion, to practice justice and charity and mercy.[21] The penalties for violation of the oath were religious penances. The knight was a man dedicated. It was this fusion of the martial and the religious which prepared the way for the Crusades, the epic adventures of the Middle Ages. When Pope Urban II, once a Cluniac monk, proclaimed the First Crusade at Clermont, in 1095, the chief inducement he offered to the Christian knights for taking part in the Crusade was an indulgence.[22]

And by Improving the Lot of the Serfs

It is not within the purpose of this chapter to go into the history of serfdom. But a reform which opened the way for serfs to develop themselves is a very important event in the history of education, and its importance is stressed by the fact that in the tenth and eleventh centuries the serfs constituted by far the largest part of the population of Europe. Old Roman Laws[23] had forbidden rural slaves to be removed from the land of their origin. The barbarians, besides adding greatly to the number of slaves, suppressed these laws. The Church revived them for her own serfs, and gradually, both by the influence of her example and by the persuasions of Cluniac monks in the various regional councils, got the feudal lords to accept them.[24] Seebohm points out that serfdom was a transitional stage between slavery and freedom.[25] And it was the application of Christian principles to feudal society by and through Cluny which furthered that transition. Peter the Venerable, Abbot of Cluny, replying to the Apologia of St. Bernard in 1125, says: "We look upon our serfs, not as slaves and handmaids, but as brothers and sisters."[26] The way to freedom opened through Christian charity and the Christian sense of spiritual equality. In the twelfth century Walter Mapes could say that the villeins were educating their ignoble offspring in the liberal arts.[27] In France and Italy serfs increasingly gained their freedom during the eleventh and twelfth centuries, and serfdom had practically disappeared by the end of the fourteenth century. There were, obviously, many causes at work in this change;[28] but a notable impetus comes from Cluny.[29]

A Restored Society Ready for Intellectual Development

It is unwise to forget that all educational development is not merely slow (and not always in a forward direction), but that it is continuous, linking a constant succession of causes and effects. A mere handful of intelligent and energetic men may speed up the process, but only when the mass of men are ready to follow their leadership. It is this fact which at times tempts the historian of education to despair; he can never catch and put upon paper adequately that most elusive yet most important element of development, the temper and spirit of the people. Now it was that temper of the age which Cluny had changed, in every part of society, from the highest nobles to the lowest of the peasants. It is perhaps significant that schools begin to multiply in the eleventh century; but it is more significant that there is a growth of interest in things of the mind. Yet it appalls one to find modern historians sneering at the fact that great part of that interest should concern itself with revealed truths. The Christian ideal was finding a home again in the family, that basis of all society. The home life of Guibert de Nogent, appealingly described in his autobiography,[30] was typical of an increasingly large number of homes. Family life began to take precedence over the business of war. It is a sort of symbol of the age that within little more than a long lifetime, the pirate Normans became builders, founding between 1050 and 1125 a new and admirable style of architecture. Christendom was beginning again to indulge in the luxury of thinking.

Material for Intellectual Revival Supplied in Part by Saracens

Left to itself, Europe would have revived the arts and sciences. The peoples who created Gothic architectures and sculpture, who made the glass of the marvelous windows of Saint-Denis and Charters, who determined the diatonic scale in music, who invented the mariner's compass, and who wove the tapestry of Bayeux, were not intellectually or aesthetically helpless, to say the least. Gerbert, born about 950, who became a monk in the Benedictine abbey of St. Geraldus at Aurillac in Auvergne, might seem to sum up in his one person the learning of the time; and a study of his extant writings, and the life by his disciple Richer, make clear that that learning was not inconsiderable. [31] The ferment of thought in Europe was vigorous.[32] But it moved more swiftly for the help it got from a strange source, the once threatening Saracens or Moors of Spain.

The contribution of the Saracens should not be undervalued. It consisted chiefly in reintroducing to Europe the learning of the Greeks, particularly their writings in philosophy and medicine, and in bringing to Western civilization the great gift of the Hindu numerals and some of their mathematics.[33] But two facts should be remembered, in this connection. The first is that the new acquaintance with foreign learning would have been useless unless the peoples of Europe were actively ready to profit by it. Mere exposure to learning is not education (though many schools are conducted on the supposition that it is). It was what

Europeans of the eleventh and twelfth centuries brought to the new learning that determined its value to them.[34] The second fact is that, at the very time that Europe was entering upon the astonishing intellectual development of the thirteenth century, the Saracens were slipping back into stagnation and decay.

The Strange History of Learning amongst the Saracens

Lack of space forbids going into any study of the education of the Saracens; but it is important to our history to consider their learning. Mohammed, an illiterate man, founded his religion about 621 A.D. It was not an intellectual movement, but one of militant fanaticism; the Koran, committed to writing only after the death of Mohammed, is a jumble of disconnected sentences. The new religion spread rapidly. Before the close of the seventh century it came into contact with the cultured people of Syria. Some Nestorian monks had made a Syriac versions of the writings of Aristotle and the neo-Platonists and some of the Greek authorities on medicine; these they again translated into Arabic. When, about 750, the Khalifate was moved to Baghdad, some of the influential Moslems favored the new learning. Harun-al-Raschid, Khalif from 786 to 809, urged the establishment of schools. His son, Al-Mamum, who ruled from 813 to 833, founded a great school, with a library and observatory, at Baghdad.[35] A small number of Moslems developed enthusiasm for study. They borrowed a good deal in mathematics from the Hindus, including, of course, their convenient system of numerals; which we today commonly call Arabic. But the enthusiasm never spread widely. The mass of the people looked upon it with suspicion and aversion. Nevertheless it persisted for centuries, based chiefly upon two noble interests: an interest in medicine, and a desire to rationalize the fanatic vagaries of Mohammedanism. Both these pursuits reached their best development, in the East, in Avicenna (Ibn Sina) a Persian physician, who was born in 980 and died in 1037. However, the popular opposition to learning had been growing, and was driving the scholars out of the East into the new Khalifate of Spain. In the East the movement dwindled into the writing of silly chronicles and lascivious romances. In its new home in Spain it thrived mightly. It became the fashion for men of wealth to collect manuscripts[36] and to act as patrons to scholars. Most of the learning was centered in the study of medicine, based upon the writings of Galen and later of Hippocrates and Aristotle. But the medical studies involved chemistry and even astrology: in the search for the elixir of life and the philosopher's stone and a control of the influence of the stars. These researches often carried keen minds into real philosophy and real discoveries in the sciences. Geber discovered nitric acid, and Rhazes sulphuric acid. Back in the time of Al-Mamum, Ptolemy's geography and astronomy had been translated into Arabic as the Almagest; and in 1196 Geber had built an observatory in Seville and made real developments in astronomy. Very many of the so-called 'Arabian physicians' were not Arabs, but jews; and it was a group of Jewish scholars who founded the famous school of medicine Montpellier, about 1090. The Moors of Spain were proud of their scholars as physicians, but began to look askance at them when they went into the study of philosophy. The greatest of their philosophers, Averroes (Ibn Roshd) was driven into exile before his death in 1198. The Jews received him and befriended him. After his death, the orthodox opposition to philosophical study triumphed; and in fact all zeal for learning began to die out amongst the Moors of Spain, as it had already died in the East.

How the Saracen Learning Came into Europe

From the tenth to the close of the twelfth centuries, the peoples of western Europe had many contacts with the Saracenic learning developed in Spain. Perhaps the first to be noted is that which came through the Moorish physicians, who were welcomed throughout Europe. Although their primary concern was with medicine, many of them had picked up no small smattering of other sciences. They impressed the awakening intellects of Europe, and were able to give them, both in speech and in writing, a great deal of information. Next, there are indications, in part historical, in part legendary, that Europeans went into Moorish Spain to study. Such a seeker after knowledge was the Englishman, Aethelhard of Bath, often called the greatest English scientist before Roger Bacon. He lived in the time of Williams Rufus, and probably went into Spain about 1090. Such were the English Robert de Tetines and the Dalmatian Herman, whom Peter of Cluny found studying astrology at Evora when he went there himself to enquire more exactly into Moslem doctrines. Peter persuaded the two to translate the Koran into Latin, in 1143. But the most important of all the media of communication between Europe and the Saracen learning were the Christian Spaniards themselves, who, in the course of the heroic reconquest of their country from the Moors, took over also the intellectual importations which the Moors had made from the Greeks and the Hindus.

The story of the reconquista has no place here. Unfortunately, though it is one of the great epic stories of the world, it has very little place in any modern writing of history. From the Battle of Covadonga, in 718, in which king Pelayo defeated the invading and conquering Saracens, and saved the little foothold of the Asturias, to the Battle of Las Navas de Toledo in 1212, covers the most inspiring part of the great struggle, which in its entirety lasted nearly eight hundred years. During the reign of Alfonso VI (1065-1109), Rodrigo Diaz, Count of Vivar, the hero whom the Spaniards call El Cid Campeador, stirred the soul of a whole people. With the capture of Toledo in 1085, the way began to open for a mastering of the Saracen learning. Christian Spain partook of the intellectual revival of all Europe, and she found at hand a considerable store of the ancient lore of the East as material to work with. Most of the men who came from various parts of Europe to profit by the Saracen learning did not actually go to Moorish teachers, but studied in Christian schools attached to monastery or cathedral. So

Gerbert had studied, at the Abbey of Cusan in Catalonia, before the close of the tenth century. At the end of the eleventh and beginning of the twelfth centuries, the monastic and cathedral schools of Spain were flourishing; and by 1150, Raymond, the Archbishop of Toledo, had gathered a group of fifty scholars, from nearly all the countries of Europe, to make a huge translation into Latin of all the learning that the Moors had compiled.[37]

Conclusion

This whole chapter is a summary. But to compact it still more, we may say that for a hundred years after the death of Charlemagne Europe was thrust farther back into barbarism by internal conflicts and foreign invasions; that it was raised from this bad state by the renewal of the Christian spirit and the revival of Roman principles of social organization, brought about largely through the Cluniac reform; that, with the restoration of some social and moral stability, the intellectual life of Europe began to function once more; and that it providentially found a rich mental provender awaiting it in the antique learning which the Saracens had so strangely carried out of the East. The twelfth century marks the definite passing of the Dark Ages, and the coming of a new civilization, as sharply characterized as has been that of the Greeks and the Romans.

Topics for Discussion

1. The training of a knight.
2. The place of women in the education of chivalry.
3. The educational function of the Jongleurs.
4. Schools in the Cluniac monasteries.
5. Gerbert and his disciples.
6. The schools of Rheims and Chartres.
7. The libraries of this period.

REFERENCES

1. Cf. Laurie, *Rise and Constitution of Universities*, Lect. III. See especially S. R. Maitland, *The Dark Ages*, Rivington, London, 1844.

2. Cf. Finlay, *Byzantine Empire*, Bk. I, p. 265.

3. The educational influence of Alfred has been as much exaggerated by some writers as has been that of Charlemagne. Historical perspective would seem to be rare. It is almost amusing to note that, school,' Alfred, when he in turn wished to establish a 'palace school,' had to send to the continent for masters: Grimbald, of St. Omer, and John, a monk of Corbie. Learning had no real foothold anywhere in that age, which needed first to be civilized before it could be interested in such things as books and schools. Alfred's 'revival' failed even more signally that Charlemagne's.

4. In case of schools, this was true until after the year 1000. Indeed, the fact is constantly made the basis of a malevolent charge that the Catholic Church in the Middle Ages held a monopoly in education. Of any monopoly by design, there is simply no evidence: beyond the essential monopoly conferred on it by its Founder, when He commissioned it to 'teach all nations,' and gave His revelation into its keeping. The monopoly in fact (i.e., that there were no other schools) is patently explained by the equally evident facts that no other organization made any attempt to establish schools.

5. Cf. Acta Conc. Metz, 909. Mansi, Vol.18. pp. 270 sqq. Odo, the second abbot of Cluny (927-42), expressly attributes the corruption of the monks to the dispersion caused by the invasions. Cf. Vita Odonis a Joanne, 3:2, Migne, P.L., 133:96.

6. Cf. H. Belloc, *The Road*, New York, 1925, pp. 147 sqq.

7. Cf. *Collationes Odonis*, Migne, P.L., 133:518 sqq.

8. Benedict of Aniane, who died in 821, had, with the aid and encouragement of Louis the Mild, reformed the monks of a number of Benedictine abbeys; but his work died with him. The changes he introduced into the Benedictine 'rule' were adopted by Berno, and made the base of his new reform. They may be read in Migne, P.L., 103:701-1380.

9. A. K. Porter, *Romanesque Sculpture on the Pilgrimage Roads*, 10 vols., Boston, 1923, recounts in detail how the influence of Cluny spread first to Burgundy, then to England, northern

Spain, the Germanies, southern Italy; and most strikingly how it passed along the great highway which led to the shrine of St. James at Compostella.

10. Under Huge, abbot from 1049 to 1109, the total number of Cluniac monks was reckoned at some ten thousand. At the general chapter of 1132, summoned by the abbot, Peter the Venerable, more than two hundred priors attended.

11. It is significant that, although Odo definitely aimed at a general reform of monasticism, and was empowered by Pope John XI in 931 (Migne, P.L., 132:1057) to receive "any monk from any monastery who should wish to pass over to your manner of living," he reformed twice as many monasteries as those which he added to the Cluny system; and although he had the backing of civil lords, he used no force, but relied upon persuasion. (See the reform of Fleury: Migne, P.L., 133:81. Vita Odonis a Joanne, 3:8.)

12. The Cluniac monasteries were placed directly under papal jurisdiction. This fact and its political consequences, in establishing an influenctial organization within the various feudal states which was free of control by those states, are of enormous importance in the social and political history of Europe. Whether men managed that new central political power well or ill in the succeeding centuries, there is no denying that in the eleventh and twelfth centuries the papal power was the great source of social unity in Europe and a most potent influence in bringing Europe out of barbarism.

13. It is stupid, furthermore, to ignore the obvious fact that moral and religious education involves a very energetic use of the intellect in grasping and applying great truths.

14. Bollandists, *Acta SS.*, 27 Febr., p. 697.

15. Mansi, *Conscilta*, Vol. 19, 89-90. It is worth remark that at this council, as also at the councils of Hery (1024) and Eine (1027) women took part. Cf. Mansi, Vol. 19, 483.

16. Mansi, Vol. 19, 267.

17. Mansi, Vol. 19, 483.

18. Mansi, Vol. 19, 593.

19. It may help us to realize the educational significance of the truce of God. If we compare the effort which brought it into existence with the efforts expended, since the World War of 1914-18, upon a covenant of peace: (1) in the conditions under

which the two have been made (a semibarbaric feudalism and a supposedly high civilization); (2) in the means employed (the universal Catholic religion, and congresses of diplomats); and (3) in the relative success of the two attempts.

20. Cf. L. Reynaud, *Les origines de Pinfluence francaise en Allemagne*, Paris, 1913, pp. 43, 339. Kenelm Digby, *The Broadstone of Honour.*

21. The distinctive education of a knight is well known. In its later development, it included an elementary training in letters and in moral conduct, then a training in the use of arms and the military art and finally training in elaborate courtesy and such graces of life as the age knew; the whole strongly pervaded by the spirit of religion. Although it was concerned with only a small percentage of the population, its influence was considerable, because that small part of society constituted the social leaders.

22. Can. 2: Quicunque pro sola devotione, non pro honoris vel pecuniae adeptione, ad liberandam ecclesiam Del Jerusalem profectus fuerit, iter illud pro omni penitentia reputetur. Mansi, *Concilia*, Vol. 20, 816.

23. Constantine in 332, Valentinian I in 377. Cf. Cod. Justin., XI, xivii, 2.

24. St. Ives of Chartres in his Decretum, collects many of the ancient canons which imposed upon churches the duty of defending the liberty of freed slaves. See particularly pars xvi, cap. 46-54 (Migna P.L., 161:915 sqq.). There is an interesting letter of Pope Geiasius (492-496) to Bishop Bonifacius, which implies that churches had even gone much further than this, and given sanctuary to rum away slaves (Migne, *P.L.*, 59:152). In the laws of St. Stephen King of Hungary (who died in 1038) there is clear evidence that the manumission of slaves was a frequent act, done out of the motive of Christian charity (Ch. xvii; Migne, *P.L.*, 151:1248). The 66th chapter of the laws of William the Conqueror, granting liberty to any serf who dwelt for a year and a day in one of the King's cities of camps, or in a walled town, is an outgrowth of the Christian practice of monasteries and churches (Cf. Migne, P.L., 149:1320). The freeing of the serfs was necessarily, and wisely a slow and gradual affair: but it would never have had its beginning except in the spirit of Christian charity. The influence of the great St. Hugh Abbot of Clunny from 1049 to 1109, in furthering the growth of this spirit both by precept and by

example, may be gathered from various details in his life, as recounted in the *Bibliotheca Cluniacensis*, pp. 413-35: 447-62; 557-60. Stubbs, in *Select Charters*, says that serfs might not become clerics or monks and quotes the Assize of Clarendon, under Henry II, of 1166. But that decision merely repeats the law of Cap. xvi. Constitution of Clarendon, 1164, which does not forbid the eradination of serfs, but only cautions that before a serf be accepted as monk or cleric due inquiry be made to safeguard the rights of his feudal lord. The text is: "Prohibet dominus rex ne monachi canonici vel aliqua domus religionum recipiat aliquem de popul minuto in monachum vel canonicum vel fratrem, donec sciatur of Quali testimonio ipse fuerit, nist ipse fuerit infirmus ad mortem". which latter case, of course, the rights of the serf's lord were on the verge of eternal cancellation.

25. *The English Vilage Community*, London, 1833, Vol. 8, pp. 252-316. He is in agreement with Fustel de Coulanges, *Histoire des Institutions Politiques de P Ancienne France*, Paris, 1901.

26. Epist., 28: Migne, *P.L.*, 189:146.

27. Nicholas Breakspear, who, as Adrian IV, was the only English pope, had been a serf. He was pope from 1154 to 1159. See his Life by Cardinal Boso, in Migne, *P.L.*, 188:1351-60.

28. Many writers have exaggerated the influence exerted through all the developments of the tenth century by the superstitious fear that the year 1000 was to see the end of the world. Contemporary records make clear that, though this fear was widespread amongst the peasants and the more ignorant of the nobility and clergy, it had little hold or influence upon the men who wre shaping the course of events, and its influence upon the common people was neither profound nor lasting. See for instance, the quarrel between Arnulph and Gerbert (five years later to be the first French Pope, under the title of Sylvester II) over the see of Rheims, and the decision against Gerbert by Pope Gregory V in 996 (Mansi, *Concilia*, Vol. 19, 103 sqq. and 173 sqq.). See also the Life and Letters of Sylvester II, Popefrom 999 to 1003, in Mansi, Vol. 19, 240 sqq.; especially Sylvester's letter of 999, proposing to arm Christendom in a crusade to deliver the holy sepulchre from the hands of the Moslems, in Muratori, Script. Vol. 3, p. 400, and Recueil des historiens des Gaules, etc.,Plame, Paris, 1874, Vol. 10, p. 426. In the same way, the English monastic and educational reforms of Sts. Dunstan, Ethelwold, and Oswald, and the famous Abbot of Fleury, during the last quarter of the

tenth century, are the work of forward-looking men, not of men paralyzed by fear of an impending end of the world. In the eighteen years he was Archbishop of Canterbury (he died in 978), St. Dunstan founded or restored more than forty abbeys, reformed large numbers of the clergy, and to some extent revived the system of parish elementary schools which had been destroyed in the Danish invasions. See also the Annales of Thietmar of Meres burg, for the Germanies, referring to the year 1000; in Pertz, Mos Germ. Hist., Vol. 5; and the life of Bornward, Bishop of Hildeshelm from 992 to 1021, by his teacher Thangmar, in Migne, *P.L.,* Vol. 140. *The Chronicon Vanetum* of John the Deacon, in Migne, *P.L.* 139:871, covers the period to 1008. The only man of note who seems to have been affected by the popular fear was the boy-Emperor, Otho III, crowned in 996, poisoned in 1002 by his mistress, Stephania, whose husband he had ordered beheaded in 997 for a conspiracy against Pope Gregory V. But Otho's age (he was only sixteen when he became emperor) may help to account for the exception.

29. There is pitiful irony in the fact that later on Cluny fell into decay, through wealth and the inertia of overgrown numbers and power. Its place was taken by the new reform of Citeaux, under the great St. Bernard. But the incomparable work of Cluny in the education of western Europe was well done before Cluny itself went the way of all human institutions.

30. *De Vita Sua sive Monodiarum;* Migne, *P.L.*, Vol. 156. It has been rather clumsily translated into English by C.C. Swinton Bland, Dution and Co., New York, 1926. See also B. Monod, *Le Moine Guibert et Son Temps,* Paris, Hachette, 1905. Gulbert was born at Clermonten Beauvaisls in 1053, died Abbot of Notre Dame de Nogent in 1124.

31. Richerus, *Historiarum Libri IV,* Migne, *P.L.*, 138:17 sqq. See especially lib. iii. Cr. also Picavet, *Gerbert, un Pape Philosophe,* Lerous, Paris, 1897.

32. Evidences of the intellectual awakening of Europe in the eleventh century are found also in the growth of scholarship outside the monastic and cathedral schools. For the first time in centuries lay teachers begin to appear and soon become rather numerous. Possibly the elevation to the papacy of Gerbert, the brilliant school teacher of Rheims, stimulated the ambition of men, and pointed to the fact that books might be as useful as the sword in achieving success. Cf. Rodulfus Glaber, *Historiarum Libri,* Migne, *P.L.*, 142:611-93. Berengar,

of unhappy fame, was one of these teachers. He was born about the year 1000. Cf. Ep. Adelman., Migne, P.L., 143:1261 sqq.

33. Von Humboldt (Cosmos, II, p. 226, note to p. 358) considers it more than probable... that the Christians in the west were familiar with Indian numerals even earlier than the Arabs," and bases his acceptance of the statement on the work of the mathematician Charles. Aperqu historique des Methodes en Geometric 1837, pp. 464-72. The question is discussed in the Comptes renderde I'Accededmte des Sciences, Vol. 8 (1839), p. 78; Vol. 9 (1839), p. 449; Vol. 16 (1843), pp. 156-73, 218-46; and Vol. 17 (1843), pp. 143-54.

34. Even in the latter half of the tenth century there are evidence of intellectual enthusiasm in the reformed monastic and cathedral schools. See, for instance, Richer's Life of Gerbert, in Pertz, Monkmenta Germaniae Historica, Vol. 3, and Richeri, Hist., Lib. iii, 47-53 in Migne, 138:102-05, where Gerbert is said to have taught rhetoric from the classic Latin poets, dramatists and satirists, and astronomy with the aid of globes, showing a knowledge of the sphericity of the earth, the elliptical planes, and the movements of the stars. Gerbert's pupil. Fulbert, Bishop of Chartres from 1006 to 1028, and a friend of Odilo of Cluny, founded a great school, or rather re-established as old school, at Chartres, which was deservedly famous. Cf. Les. Ecoles de Chartres au Moyen Age, by the Abbe Clerval (Memoires de li Societe archeologique d'Eure-et-Loir, Vol. 11, 1895).

35. By way of comparison, it may be pointed out that Al-Mamum's astronomers never attained to an accuracy in determining the solar year equal to the work of the Etruscans (Cf. Niebuhr. *Hist. of Rome*, Vol. 1, 274) or the even better work of the Mayas in America (Cf. Humboldt, *Vues des Cordilires et Monuments des Peuples indigenes de L'Amerique*, p. 125).

36. The Khalif Al-Hakem II (961-76) is said to have gathered together in his library at Cordoya 600,000 books and manuscripts. Though this is a manifest exaggeration, the legend testifies to the prestige attaching to the possession of a great library.

37. It must not be forgotten that, during the twelfth century, the Crusades brought western Europe into direct touch with the Greeks and other peoples of the East, and were the occasion of at least some slight infiltration of learning into the West. But that, at best, was a thin stream. More came by way of

Northern Africa and Sicilly. But Spain was the chief channel. Roger Bacon (Opus Majus, pars I, Cap. xiii) credits the introduction of Aristotle to the version by Michael Scot which appeared in 1230. However, the greatest of the translators was jGerard of Cremona, who was born in 1114 and died at Toledo in 1187, and who turned into Latin more than eighty Arabic works; three on logic a half dozen on mathematics, a score or more on astronomy and other sciences, and a long list of medical treatises.

4

Pride and Prejudice in Education

"The infinitely little have a pride infinitely great."

—**Voltaire**

"Pride ruined the angel."

—**Emerson**

Everybody will agree with the saying, that one task, perhaps one of the most important tasks, of the school is to dispel prejudice and encourage the appeal to reason in all that concerns the affairs of our private or public lives. A type of psychology which in the last many decades has made a great stir in the world is that which attributes all, or by far the larger part, of our actions to the impelling power of our brute instincts, and yields to the reason only the function of finding means to those ends, or even of finding excuses to offer to the conscious self for following those ends. The ideas themselves are not new. What was new in Freud's teaching was the tremendous emphasis on them, the invention of a technical terminology by which to discuss the insides of our minds where these dark forces held sway, and of a technique for dragging the conflicts there taking place into the light of day, i.e. of the reason.

"Boys are just like people", says Aunt Sarah in Booth Tarkington's *Penrod*, "only they're not quite so awful because they haven't learned to cover themselves all over with little pretences. When Penrod grows up he'll be just the same as he is now, except that whenever he does what he wants to do he'll tell himself and other people a little story about it to make his reason for doing it seem nice and pretty and noble."

"No, I won't", said Penrod suddenly.

"There's one cookie left", observed Aunt Sarah. "Are you going to eat it?"

"Well", said her great-nephew thoughtfully, "I guess I'd better."

"Why?" asked the old lady. "Why do you guess you'd better?"

"Well", said Penrod, with a full mouth, "it might get all dried up if nobody took it, and get thrown out and wasted."

"You're beginning finely", Mrs. Green remarked.

But Penrod would almost certainly, could be have understood what his great-aunt was getting at, have protested that he really had felt that way, and had not at all wanted to eat the cookie because he was greedy, and he would very probably have believed himself. What he did in a small matter we all do in great matters, and rationalize our prejudices by giving excellent reasons for them, deceiving ourselves in the process, of which we are in the majority of cases quite unconscious.

As educators, we have to decide our position as to this widespread tendency: and it is very difficult to do. There is in the first place the question whether we ourselves possess prejudices which by example and precept we are passing on to our pupils. And after we have discovered some of these prejudices, there is the still more conscience-racking problem if, as is sometimes the case, the prejudices seem to us to serve a highly useful and commendable purpose which would not be served were we to attempt to get the same result by appeals to reason and fail.

The subject in which difficulties of these kinds are greatest is, of course, religion. But for that very reason the reader will permit it to be passed over here, in favour of examples less likely to wound his feelings, though I am afraid no good example will be quite free from that danger. Take national patriotism. Practically every normal person, at any rate if he has been bred in the same country as he was born in, quite naturally becomes patriotic. Patriotism is a complex sentiment, and a perfectly harmless part of the mixture is affection for the district and the country of one's infant nurture. But patriotism, quite unconsciously, takes liberties with the truth, and that is less innocuous. I have heard the Battle of Waterloo described by English teachers to English children, and (this was long before the Great War) by German teachers to German children, and it was hardly recognizable as the same battle. An uneasy feeling is left in one's mind that perhaps it was not quite like either of the descriptions. Remember that, I am firmly convinced, the teacher of the one nationality was as certain of his impartiality as the teacher of the other. Unluckily, I have not heard that battle described by a French teacher to French children. Or, to come nearer home, I have heard a lesson on William Wallace in a Northumberland village, where that doughty Scot had in his time locked the inhabitants into the church and fired it. The impression left by that lesson was different from that left by lessons on the same hero in Scotland. Probably the Scottish lessons are the more true, for the national saviour rather than the ruthless raider is the predominant personality in him. But my point is that the angles of view were honestly different. Moreover, it is possible to run to the opposite extreme and praise "every century but this and every country but his own", as Gilbert sang. And if one takes refuge in the *via media* in all things, in the first place one becomes a very wishy-washy sort of person, and secondly, one end of the controversy, as Aristotle himself said, is commonly less wrong than the other.

Of course, the difficulties we speak of are not met with

equally by teachers of different subjects, though that does not at bottom affect the matter much, for it is the general attitude of a teacher to affairs in general—moral, religious, political, public—which cannot fail to communicate itself in some sort to those with whom he comes in contact. But admittedly the teacher of mathematics does not usually convey serious prejudices in that subject, which is one on which differences of faith are uncommon, though not entirely unknown. And the striking, continuous, and continuing advances made by the natural sciecnces in the last hundred years or so are certainly attributable to the comparative willingness of men in that province of thought to ascertain and be led by the whole set of facts. Many, like J. Harvey Robinson in *The Mind in the Making*, and Graham Wallas, less directly, in *The Great Society* and others of his books, have preached that the millennium would be here could we only learn to do in morals and politics what we already do in natural science. And that is the millennium towards which most honest-minded people of intelligence and with a scientific training try to help the world, often at some sacrifice to themselves. They love Plato, but truth they love more. Yet has anyone of us ever unflinchingly considered what the world would be like, at any rate in our time, if everyone could be divested of his or her prejudices?

Is truth strong enough to control the mass of mankind? Are prejudices necessary, in order that we may live in some sort of peace and unity, at least with our fellow-countrymen of the same class? Are the individual differences of intellect among normal men such that the truth to some would be meaningless nonsense to others? Is there any absolute truth anyhow, or only truth for this or that level of intellect, and are we to assume that the highest known human intellect has necessarily reached truth in anything? For that highest intellect looks on the "truth" of some lower intellects as not merely incomplete, but often actually erroneous, so why should not his be the same?

One of the best students in an essay on some subject from Plato's *Republic*, of "leaving aside the absurd myth of being fashioned of various metals in the bowels of the earth". But was it so absurd a myth? We think it showed the extreme insight of the Platonic Socrates to recognize that an appeal to reason would not be able to "sell" his *Republic* to the populace, but that some other sanction would be required. Does not Nietzsche say somewhere, "reasons make the populace suspicious"? And suppose you, reader, were faced with the prospect of bringing into actual being Plato's Republic, or, if you like, some other Utopia more acceptance to your ideals, if only you would teach some such myth, which would you choose—Plato or truth? And which, if it comes to that, are you choosing at this very moment?

Perhaps you are one of those lucky ones whose faith, patriotism, political beliefs, and all the rest are unshakable. In that case you probably owe your happiness to the inculcation of prejudices by your teachers of various sorts, for it is unlikely that your unshakable opinions are true. Many such unshakable people can be assembled and as they hold many different opinions it is certain that the majority must be holding opinions which are untrue, unless, indeed, you adopt a relative definition of truth such as was hinted at above. At any rate, their opinions cannot be simultaneously true.

For ourselves, though we confess to almost daily hypocrisy in one thing or another, we believe in our heart in truth, and that, unless this Creation were that of some cunning devil, truth and the world's happiness must in the long run coincide in direction. It is just cowardice that makes us, perhaps all of us, hypocrites now and then of often. But there may have been high-minded deliberate hypocrites in the world's history, who taught what they did not believe for the sake of the happiness of others, not their own; and if there were or are such, we honour them. The ordinary teacher had better stick to truth. And though he should show ordinary common sense in waiting till he is sure it is truth, and not a passing fancy, he should not, on the other hand, shelter himself too long under that excuse.

On the other side of the question, let us not forget that reason is a cold-blooded sort of thing, and that no cruelty can be more abhorrent than that of an inhuman logically minded monster. Portia brought logic to her aid and outdid Shylock on his own ground, but we do not approve because of that, but because we feel our instinct rebelling against the "just" verdict. A perfectly watertight and logical system of discipline in school or state, executed mechanically, can have, in spite of its perfection or because of it, the most disastrous consequences, while a much less logical system, administered with mercy and a little elasticity, together with a sense of humour, will succeed. Presumably that is because the logic and rationality of the former is not really perfect, but the fact remains that people, motivated entirely by their reasons, have a tendency to lose their sense of relative values and to make mountains out of molehills.

There have been periods in the world's history when reason was more in favour, and in others prejudice and tradition. Some centuries in Greece, some in Rome, were ages of reason; the Enlightenment in the eighteenth century, the notorious "Age of Reason" itself, the last quarter of the last century, seem to me to have been "rational" periods. To-day, there seem to be signs of a reaction. In Germany, at least, one reads often attacks on *Rationalismus* which appears to be associated with the time of discipline and anti-individualism of the pre-war period. Reason appears to have been now claimed as an ally, now feared as an enemy, by followers of freedom. And it must be confessed that the epochs of the supremacy of reason have nearly all something about them which repels taste and the moral sense.

One thing, however, seems clear, that prejudices which are born of misrepresentation and actual untruth must most certainly be evil; and such prejudices are only possible of growth where there is ignorance of nation concerning nation, of class concerning class, of religion concerning religion. The peculiar difficulty of the educationist about matters of opinion and belief is that he is faced with the dilemma, either of using the educational period consciously or unconsciously to inculcate those prejudices which he thinks right, or of placing upon the immature child the responsibility, which in some matters is tremendous, of making a choice for himself. But is there really such a clear cut distinction? Is there not the possible course of making the school a microcosm of the outer world, containing the children of all opinions of parents, and carefully refraining from calling attention to these differences of opinion until they actually arise in the life of the school in some childish form, when there might be discussion and decision by the children about the particular point, which would not as a rule be a major clash of opinion, but would serve as a training in seeing the point of view of others while adhering to such of one's own opinions as seemed to an honest mind to stand the test of criticism by one's fellows and one's own conscience.

That school should be such a microcosm, however, implies that it should certain children of all classes and even of all religions. Against the practicability of such a system, however, there is a great body of public opinion, and there are apart from prejudice other practical difficulties which cannot be minimized.

The aims of education which are explicitly enunciated by teachers, parents, and members of the public are not always the real purposes which actuate them when they take part in the process of education: and it cannot be denied that one of the motives which influence the choice of a place of education is the desire to share in the social standing conferred by a certain school. Teachers are in many cases swayed by a similar motive in applying for posts, or head masters in deciding upon curricula and time-tables: while the general public is not unaware that school A and school B differ socially; and shows a tendency to be divided into those who think B plebeian and those who call A snobbish, among which latter class are, it is to be feared, some who would join the other party if they could; I have no desire to accuse the whole of society of hypocrisy in this matter, but only to express my belief that all of us are in danger of being influenced by such considerations without admitting it to ourselves or possibly even being conscious of it.

There are in Great Britain several kinds of educational ladder, which are largely of different historical origin, and which serve different purposes; it is fairly easy to distinguish three of these. First, there are the public schools in the narrower sense, mainly residential in character, schools like Eton, Winchester, Haileybury, Oundle. These receive boys from preparatory schools, which often are also residential, and large numbers of their scholars, probably a substantial majority, pass on to a university on to the army or navy. There are two streams ascending this ladder: one composed of boys of very considerable intellectual ability, probably all over 125 in "intelligence quotient" (an IQ is the percentage which mental age bears to chronological age, so that 100 is normal) who win an almost free education (after the preparatory-school stage) in severe competition; the other composed of boys whose parents can pay the whole bill, i.e. parents who are either very well-to-do or, being moderately so, are willing to deny themselves luxuries and even necessaries to enable their children to have the advantages of a public-school education. This second stream of boys is not necessarily devoid of brains. On the contrary, it also almost certainly averages distinctly over normal intelligence, say about 110 I.Q., and undoubtedly contains some individuals as able as are the competitive "scholars". But it also carries a certain number of boys below average intelligence, or, at least, we may strongly suspect this.

A second ladder is that formed by grammar schools for boys and high schools for girls, which are not usually residential, and which keep their pupils from quite an early age (say nine years or less; before nine such children are often at small private schools in ordinary houses) to 17 or 18. Many, however, drop out at an early age, and the percentage of those passing on to a university is very much smaller than is the case in the public schools. The line of demarcation, however, is not always easy to follow: and, on the other side, many of these schools (an increasing number) form a part of the third great ladder, that which is the official educational system of the country, and whose until members (since the natural name for them, and that actually used in Scotland, has been already employed for the public schools) we may call state schools. State schools are mainly elementary schools and secondary schools; and there are also central schools, technical schools, higher elementary schools, advanced divisions (in Scotland) and other branches. The organization is at present (1928) on the eve of considerable developments and changes in nomenclature, and in the co-ordination of its different parts of which notice is taken elsewhere.

The elementary schools are entirely supported by public money, approximately one-half coming from the central Treasury in London and one-half from local rates. The secondary schools are supported by approximately equal contributions from three sources, namely the central Treasury, the local rates, and the scholars' fees. But always 25 per cent of the scholars have their fees remitted, and this percentage is in many instances 40 per cent and in a few 100 per cent., in which latter case the cost is again entirely borne by the public.

The numbers ascending these three ladders are very different, being smallest in the case of the public schools, and far the largest in the case of the state schools: and there is a strongly marked social distinction between them. The marks of the higher social class are in accent, behaviour, and dress; the latter, however, being less important, provided certain minimum essentials are fulfilled. Accent is indispensable, and the behaviour must conform to certain convictions, which favour a high standard of personal honour, but do not always exclude that form of departure from perfection which permits the definition of a gentleman as one who is never unintentionally offensive. To what extent is it the duty of the teacher in the state school to endeavour to give to his pupils these marks of social distinction? Of course, the true answer is that he ought not to care for these things *merely* as social badges, and ought not, on the other hand, to hold them in contempt if they have, as may be the case, true values as well as the conventional. Attention to accent, for example, is praiseworthy for other reasons; but it is very difficult to steer a true course between unworthy and snobbish motives on the one hand and disdainful neglect on the other. The teacher who holds as best he can to the *via media* can also have the consolation that attempts to put an "aristocratic" accent into the mouths of pupils are not often successful, and that were they to become successful on any large scale, and state-school children to speak just like preparatory-school children, a new distinction would assuredly be invented by the exclusive classes.

There is one nation where circumstances made it seem for a while as though the state schools would be the schools for all. In the northern states of the American Union rich and poor sat for a time on the same school bench. Even to-day in many districts the rich man's son is much more likely to attend the state school than would be the case in England: and one state actually passed a law making attendance at the state schools (and no other) compulsory. It is very possible, however, that this law was aimed as much at religious bodies as at aristocracy: and, in any case, it has been declared unconstitutional, and has not come into force. To the logic leading towards such a law we shall return presently. In default of such compulsion it is abundantly clear that social distinctions between private and state schools will continue. Whatever the defence for such may be, there cannot well be any defence for, or toleration of, social distinctions between various types of *state* school. The possibility of such distinctions is one of the great drawbacks to that system of differentiation of types of secondary school which appears to be most in favour at present in England, namely a system providing at least two, and possibly three or more, kinds of education for different kinds of children in different school buildings.

For children cannot all profit by the same kind of education. Their minds are, at least, as different as their bodies. Nature, fresh air, good food, suitable exercise, can influence a man's physique, but cannot add a cubit to his stature. Some of us are short and some of us are tall, some blue-eyed and some brown: and we have equally variegated minds. Schooling can do for the mind what food and exercise can do for the body, but no more. To a child's mental stature schooling may add an inch, but not a cubit. There are irreducible differences left when all is said and done, and these differences are such that no one type of schooling will suit all children. The differences show more and more as the children grow older: so that while the kindergarten may do for all, and the junior school with devices such as "multiple tracks" may do for most, for the adolescent decidedly different kinds of treatment are imperative; and in England these are given in different kinds of school. *The difficulty is to create the different types of school side by side on a social equality, without permitting them to appear higher or lower in a scale of snobbishness.* The difficulty arises because one of the types of school will resemble the present socially favoured schools more than other types will: because one type of school will suit few, and another will suit many, and rarity causes a rise in value; and because graduates of one type of school will tend to obtain in after-life better-paid posts than those of another type.

The present type of secondary school has a bookish and abstract curriculum; it looks towards the university and the professions, and it gives its pupils an education which is almost entirely useless if they do not go to a university or into a profession. There is a perfectly definite need for such a curriculum, but it will never suit more than about 10 per cent or so of the child population, or, since this is a difficult matter on which to express an opinion, let us say, at any rate, never more than a quarter; and this fraction, whatever it is, ought *all* to go on to universities or other forms of higher education, whereas to-day only a very small proportion do so. The 10 per cent (or more) of our children taking such a curriculum ought to be more carefully selected than is the case to-day; everyone of them ought to have an intelligence quotient of at least 115 (if one-quarter were to be chosen it would fall below that) and an interest in abstract studies; and their way through the university ought to be made possible even if they are poor.

But they ought not to be considered *superior* to the 90 per cent. To say that a child is intelligent is not a compliment, it is a description. The child cannot help being intelligent or unintelligent, as the case may be, and deserves no more credit for it than for his blue eyes or his snub nose. He deserves credit or discredit, I think, for his use or misuse of his intelligence; for though some would say that even here *tout comprendre c'est tout pardonner*, yet to pardon need not mean to condone.

But if these clever children are segregated, as at present in England, into separate schools, while their less intelligent brethren are provided with other types of curriculum in other schools, it will be almost, probably quite, impossible to prevent social distinctions accompanying the distinction of type of mind. And this is why it is worthwhile considering whether such segregation is really necessary. The arguments in its favour are very strong. They overlap; but one can distinguish the arguments of efficiency, of economy, of close personal influence, of *esprit de corps*, even arguments of justice and equity. The separate secondary school is very efficient in attaining its narrow aim. No doubt it is easy to point to faults and weaknesses, but they are not caused by the fact of segregation, which is what we are at present discussing. Secondary schools have been the more efficient the more they have attend strictly to their own business. The German pre-war *Gymnasium*, for example, was extremely efficient, even without the advantage of a widely cast net of selection from the primary schools, which ought to make a still higher standard attainable. In a school which catered not only for the demands of the university and the professions, but also for those of commerce, of art, of craft, and of the factory, it is very doubtful whether the same standard of efficiency could be reached which is attained to-day in separate secondary schools, commercial central schools, art schools, technical schools. If one school were to attempt all these various tasks, it could not have the "atmosphere" which helps to educate in each of the separate schools. The ordinary process of organization would seem to lead to such separate institutions.

The economy argument is double-edged. It is probably easier to make out a case for the cheapness of the "comprehensive high school", where all these courses would be under one roof, than for the separate schools, if this comprehensive school were allowed to grow in size. But the argument of limiting the school so that the head master can know personally all the scholars makes a really large school impossible for those who consider this important, and then economy steps in favour of separate schools; for a small and intellectually mixed school would need too many kinds of classes and masters to pay, unless indeed, the intellectual standard were so lowered that one course served for all, which is contrary to our whole hypothesis. Here, too, appears the "justice" argument, though it is not often heard in our country, where injustice is usually assumed to be done only to the poor and ignorant. In America, however, there is sometimes heard the saying, "A boy is entitled to his fair chance, *even if* he is of superior intelligence". The suggestion is that in a high school for all the general intellectual level is so lowered that the cleverer are handicapped, and are not receiving the kind of mental pabulum which is their due, that, in fact, they are being starved. While this, of course, need not be the case in a large and well-classified school with different kinds of courses for each category of pupil, it is certainly a danger if the schools must be small, and therefore cannot be well classified. *Ergo*, separate schools.

The esprit de corps argument is a strong one, but is exactly why some people object to the separate schools for different intellectual levels: for *esprit de corps*, like fire, is a good servant but a bad master. Looked at with other eyes, it easily can be called class-consciousness, or snobbishness, or parochialism.

There is only one argument on the other side, but it is one to be given very serious consideration; that the social solidarity of the whole nation is more important than any of the defects to which a comprehensive high school may be subject, and which may in any case be ameliorated if not even abolished. To have memories of life together in common, to have worn the same school cap, have played for the same team, will mean much for men and women even although they may not at school have been of the same intellectual level, and may have enjoyed different courses. And in a comprehensive school, under one head, there are many more chances of transferring a child from one course to another, if he be found to possess talent of a kind not at first suspected; and thus the nightmare of being tested and judged once and for all at the tender age of 11, and made or marred for life, will be removed for good.

If we turn back for a while from the education of children over 11, and let our minds dwell on our present problem as it concerns education before that age, we are at once attracted by the movement in Germany since the Revolution of 1918, to establish a common school for all classes, the *Grundschule*. Any remarks during which one has occasion to speak of the educational policy of "Germany" ought, however, to be prefaced by the explanation that the old Germany left this subject definitely to the separate kingdoms of which it was composed, and had no Imperial law of education. And even in the new Germany, although education is now mentioned in the constitution, only rather general directions are given to which the regulations of the separate components of the Reich must conform, so that nothing can be said to apply without qualification to the whole country. With this caution, however, it may be said that Germany now has a compulsory common school for the first four years of school-life, to which all children, rich and poor, dull or clever, must go; so that here certainly we have one education for all.

Even in Germany, however, there remain distinctions, we do not refer to the possibilities of evading the new law by obtaining medical certificates stating that the child's health makes a tutor at home imperative, or anything of that sort. No doubt such devices will in time be made impossible except in genuine cases. but even where you have a common school with compulsory attendance, there will, of course, be social distinctions between a school in one district and that in another. This can hardly be laid at the door of the educational administration, but is rather another way of stating the larger fact that there are social distinctions in the world outside the school which lead to the segregation of classes in certain quarters of a city.

Above the age of 10 or 11, however, Germany, too, divides its children into categories attending at different buildings. There are some exceptions to this, such as are provided by the existence of the so-called *Aufbauschulen*, and by the fact that in some parts of the German-speaking world the *Grundschule* itself lasts for five or six years (Switzerland and Austria). But on the whole the Old World makes the separation referred to, either from the beginning or after 11.

Only in North America is the passage from primary to secondary education unaccompanied by this phenomenon. There, although again one has to remember that each state is a law unto itself, there is, on the whole, a smooth passage up the whole school, and usually up the same school in the same building, for all categories. That this is the cause of the alleged backwardness, in an intellectual sense, of the schools of the United States of America is possible. But it does at least conform to the democratic demand for an avoidance, among the children, of those distinctions which are, it would seem, inevitable among adults, but which may be even among adults confined to distinctions of rank and fortune only and not complicated by that greater possibility of misunderstanding resulting from separate lives during school-days.

The question whether there is really at the age of 11 or 12 any crisis in the life of a child which demands a bifurcation of the educational path is one which all do not answer in the same way. The recent pamphlet (1928) of the English Board of Education considers that such a change is needed, and the arguments in its favour are given in another chapter. But others have urged that the crisis is not so much in the life of the child as in the mind of the administrator, who finds at that age the difficulty of proper classification of children of different intelligence becoming acute, and determines his policy accordingly. The American plan, quite apart from the question of the comprehensive high school, has another suggestion to offer. There, instead of a snapshot examination which at 11 decides the course which a child shall thereafter follow, they have the institution of the junior high school, which is designedly a trying out period of three years; after which, in the senior high school, the different courses are followed, upon which by trial and by advice the child and the parents have decided as the three junior high school years passed.

The junior high school differs from an English central or modern school, or from a Scottish advanced division, in that *all* the children pass through it. It is not an alternative to the secondary school, but is the porch leading to it. It has some resemblance to the German *Aufbauschule*, which also postpones the decision to diverge irrevocably into academic or less abstract work.

If we may look back and summarize at this point, we see that the problem is one of reconciling the fact of inborn differences both of physique, temperament, and intelligence with the democratic demand for equality. In certain senses no political or ethical creed can make people equal in these matters more than in height or colour. But the demand for equality of opportunity is one to which everyone feels his heart respond. At what point in a person's life has he had his opportunity? At some point even the most radical thinker, in the most Utopian of states, would agree, presumably, that different individuals must take up different kinds of work. The educational tendency of the last quarter century has been to fix this point, this first critical point in the life of a child of the people, at 11 or thereabouts. England does so perhaps most decidedly; Germany almost equally so. Scotland is less definite, and gives several chances, up to 13, for a child to "qualify", as they call it, and in theory at least makes the choice of kind of education, after qualifying, depend on the wish of the family, and not on how well the child has passed the qualifying examination. America passes the scholar from the primary grades into the junior high school grades with little, if any, more fuss than it passes from grade 3 (say) into grade 4; and uses the junior high school as a more leisurely deciding period as to the future.

5

Education and the Function of the School

As a natural phenomenon the whole of the environment is the instrument of man's education in the widest sense. But in that environment certain factors are worth distinction as being more particularly concerned: the home, the school, the church, the press, the vocation, public life, amusements, and hobbies. The home is most influential during infancy, school during childhood, the vocation and amusements during early manhood, the press, public life, and the church during middle age. We have not mentioned books; for books are used as a tool by all other agencies. Yet for some men they become an independent element of immense significance.

Of these factors the only one which is concerned solely with education and with nothing else is the school, by which we mean the whole educational machine from kindergarten to postgraduate university course. The school might, therefore, reasonably be expected to endeavour to coordinate the other factors, to see that overlapping is avoided and gaps filled out. With one of these other influence, indeed, cooperation has become peculiarly difficult, for in the warring of the sects it has been found in some countries impossible, and in all difficult, for the schools supported by public money to be associated with the teaching of religious dogma.

The task of the school has been variously interpreted and in these differences lie the characteristic traits of schools of different nations and of different epochs. The prevailing tendency of state schools is to give intellectual training to a preponderating extent. The school is taken to be a place where first reading, writing, and arithmetic are learned, and then other studies. Discipline and school tone are valued, but mainly as being necessary for that intellectual training. Now there is no doubt that intellectual training, in the sense of book-learning and abstract reasoning, is the task which can least successfully be cared for by the other educational influences. And in decades when there have been large numbers of illiterates in the population, it has been the "learning" the school can give which has been valued, and rightly so. Where there are no schools, there may yet be highly developed skill in craftsmanship, there may yet be fine character training, there may even be traditional learning passed on by word of mouth: but there will not, as a rule, be the ability to read. Without schools, the children of illiterate parents will grow up as illiterates, and some children of literate parents will do so also, and so illiteracy will grow. A civilization in which a majority of the citizens is unable to read in nowadays unthinkable, even though cynics may pretend to wish for it. And so in a sense the essential task of the school, the task which no other agency carries out under usual conditions, is to teach its pupils to read and to know good books. How narrow an aim this can become we shall not deny, and that it is far from being the most important task of the school we shall indeed presently urge; but it seems to be its unique and essential task.

We must not confuse the importance of a task with its uniqueness. The essential duties in life of John Jones, a crossing-sweeper, those which define him and distinguish him from other men, are those of his vocation as a crossing-sweeper. But his most important function in life may be something quite different, perhaps to rear little Jack Jones, who is one day to write an imperishable poem. It is more important for a crossing-sweeper to tell the truth than to sweep his crossing: but the latter is his essential, characteristic function. So with the school. Its most important functions may not be to teach reading and writing. But those are its peculiar functions which are not otherwise cared for in the community, except in very small measure, for not many children are taught to read in the home or learn by the observation of street notices. Quibblers may report that it is possible to imagine, or to point to, schools which do not teach reading and writing even in the widest sense. But practically all schools do so.

In commercial circles a common criticism of the schools has been, for certainly twenty years and perhaps more, that they no longer attend to the three R's thoroughly as in the good old days, but fritter their time away with all kinds of fancy subjects, such as nature study or European History or folk-dances. This criticism is in part, but only in part, justified. To a considerable extent, however, it is illusory, or misinformed, or ill-conceived. It is illusory because it is partly based on the very common human weakness of glorifying the days of one's own generation and belittling the new, and partly because it takes little or no account of the very much higher percentage of the population who are now literate, and the fact that all children now pass through school and not, as formerly, only those who themselves or through their parents had a desire for it. It is misinformed as to the actual extent of weakness in the three R's, and as to the relative accuracy in spelling, simple arithmetic, etc., of children of to-day and yesterday, and also as to the school programmes. For those critics do not always stop to think that reading is not a thing which can be taught without reading something, and that this something might as well be nature study or European History if those are interesting to the children: in short, that many of the so-called fancy lessons are in fact lessons in reading and writing, if not in arithmetic. And it is ill-conceived, for there is no doubt in the minds of most who are in the best position to judge children, that were the schools to direct their energies exclusively to grinding up the three R's, commercial houses would rapidly find their young clerks much less employable than at present.

But there is, nevertheless, an element of justice in the criticism, and it is worth while considering how the element of weakness thus disclosed may be strengthened. The cause is, as the critics rightly see, the greater width of the curriculum today. As one subject after another has claimed a place in the curriculum, there has been little or no discrimination between the subjects as to the manner in which they should be treated. They have too much been taken as separate subjects, and the same standards of accuracy have been demanded in all. In several quarters, however, notably in America,[1] where the disease is worse, it has been urged that some subjects are to be completely mastered, while others do not need the application of rigid standards of achievement, but rather are to be enjoyed as expressing the personality of the pupils, giving opportunity for cooperative work not possible in the individual mastery subjects, and supplying incentives for the study of the latter.

Working on these lines, it is conceivable that a committee of teachers and employers might decide just what parts of three R's and of knowledge subjects like geography and history are really essential to all normal children, and what standards could reasonably be exacted in these at each age. It would be found that these minimum essentials were a good deal less than is commonly realized. The kind of arithmetical sum, for example, which actually meets a boy or girl in the course of employment is not, as a rule, difficult, but requires absolute accuracy. That accuracy, in those simple sums, employers are entitled to exact from the product of the schools, and similarly with spelling and reading. More than this they are not entitled to require from every child. And in only a part of the school-day, if a determined attack was made on accuracy for that period, the necessary standards could be reached. It would not be necessary to keep every child at this work equally long. Some would finish and get away to their expression work sooner than others. But all would have to master each step and achieve the standard accuracy and speed in the fundamental operations of the tool subjects. This done, let the rest of the day be spent on education rather than training. Both sides of school work are equally valuable, and, moreover, the other lessons could be made to supply incentives to keep the mastery subjects up to the mark, both because the child could not take its place among its compeers unless it had learned what was required, and because the co-operatives tasks which groups of the scholars would undertake would lead to a need for those very weapons which the mastery periods were intended to polish.

It would have to be considered unprofessional in a teacher to give any drill work for accuracy in the fundamentals to children who already were up to the determined standards. Such pupils should be allowed to go on with freer work, and only tested in the required accuracies from time to time. And there would have to be a determined opposition to any attempt to make these standards anything more than really minimum essentials. So far, but so far only, the work of the school might be submitted to standardization, drill methods, and the production of results: but only on condition that the rest of the school-day, and the rest of the school work, was free from the requirement of individual results, and permitted to be enjoyable, buoyant, vital activity for the work's own sake alone.

It can, be truthfully said that many schools do to-day approximate to this solution of the difficulty of finding the *via media* between total disregard for "results" in the three R's and slavery to them.

Thus far, then, we have noted two duties of the school: to coordinate the other educational factors of the environment, and to give "book-learning"—the latter task being that for which the school in most societies was originally created, the book-learning being usually required in the service of the religion of the people, to provide a priesthood, or permit of the organization of society as it became more settled and in need of land-measures, of lawyers, of book-keepers. Now that education, at any rate, up to the end of the primary stage, is given to all children, we have to note that by giving book-learning the school enriches the whole environment, makes a wider choice of vocation possible, opens the door to the influence of the Press, and modifies every other element of the larger education.

Cooperation with the home varies a great deal with the type of school. The boarding-school almost replaces the home when it is the place of residence for eight months of the year for some six or more years of life. The state school cooperates with the home only in a limited sense. There is often a conscious effort to obtain the goodwill of parents, and to supply those elements of training which from the nature of the case and from no fault of their own the parents are unable to supply.[2] Thus there may be a direct attempt to compensate for poverty and squalor in the home by a more marked emphasis on cleanliness in the school, to displace a city slum speech by a better accent, or, where the dialect spoken is not a corrupt but merely an ancient form of English, to supplement it by the national tongue.[3] How difficult these tasks are, how strenuously they are attempted, and how little is on the average accomplished, is well-known to all who are familiar with schools. Of late years there have been formed in many schools "Parents' Associations", whose avowed object is to bring teachers and parents into closer contact, and give the latter a better understanding of and some voice in deciding the details of their children's education. Some of the meetings (usually monthly during the winter) of such an association are social in nature, at others members of the school staff explain and illustrate methods new since the parents' own school-days, and on yet others visiting educationists speak of larger movements. By these means, indeed, a form of adult education may be carried on, in which, for the sake of the children, who are its primary care, the day-school influences the older generation.

Cooperation with parents is essential, if for no other reason because the alternative is ousting the parents, and doing by means of the school many things which in simpler times were done by the home. The dangers of that are obvious, being mainly two: the danger of weakening the feeling of responsibility which all parents ought to experience, and thus replacing a very stable and certain, if nowadays somewhat inefficient, means of education (the home) by an efficient but easily destroyed means (the school), which in times of trouble, war, or political unrest might fail us; and the danger referred to below, of creating as sole means of education a closely organized institution which might be captured by some propagandist body and used for its ends, contrary to the wishes of the parents, who may be ignorant of what is going on. The advance in complexity and division of labour in our society has made education by the parents alone impossible, but care should always be taken to co-operate with them, who are a definite body in the community, not identical (especially since recent changes in the franchise) with the general body of the electorate, either municipal or national.

The difficulties and necessity of cooperation with parents, and the dangers of removing responsibility from the home, are seen very clearly in the period before the compulsory school-age of 5—a period, when, in the opinion of many, there is caused, by the largely unavoidable inefficiency of the home, a great deal of mental and physical defect which has to be fought afterwards in the school proper. Hence the urgent proposals to form nursery schools or nursery classes. But as their task, although complex, is perhaps most clearly perceived under the head of physique and health, we may postpone discussing them for a few pages. At the other end of school-life, when the pupil nears the time for going out into the world, co-operation with the parent again takes on a special form in connection with the choice of occupation. This also is discussed elsewhere.

Although the primary task of the school is to give

letters, yet this is not its most important task. That, in the opinion of many, is the training of character, and it is a duty which has been more and more thrust on the school by the changes accompanying the progress of civilization. This is one of the points strongly emphasized by Professor Kilpatrick, an avowed disciple of Dewey, whose philosophy of education forms the subject of a separate chapter, but which may be considered here as far as it concerns the present idea, that much character training, which in a simpler society was cared for by other agencies and by the general life of the community, must now, in our complex civilization, be looked after by the school, the whole atmosphere of which is thereby changed.

As a sample of the simpler society to which they look back, the American exponents of the present argument naturally turn to the life of the early colonists, especially the Pilgrim Fathers, or to the pioneer life of those who formed the vanguard of the Western Movement. For these the life of their little community was simple and open to view. It might be a single family in a lonely log cabin or a group of not very near neighbour families. In either case the tasks of life were set by stern necessity, were easily understood, and required the co-operation of all. Food was hunted by the adult males, cut up by them, cooked by the mother, for whom the fuel was naturally collected by the boys. The process was seen in its entirety, and shared in by all in their measure. Or the field was ploughed and harrowed, the seed sown, the crop harvested, ground in the family hand-mill or taken to a miller who was one of the little community and whose mill was known and understood by all, baked by the mother, and eaten with an understanding of the labours it had cost and the beneficence of Nature which had made it possible. Or again, the clothing they wore was seen in the process of manufacture, from the shearing of the sheep onward. Such a life taught self-help combined with co-operation, brought its own rewards, and punishments if it was not lived properly, and could be learned by simple participation on the part of the young, for whom it was never necessary to make artificial tasks, for an abundance, easily understood by them, and seen by them to be necessary and within their powers, arose in the daily life of the community.

To contrary, however, the life of a child in such a community with his life in a modern centre of civilization, and to make the contrast most striking, take the most extreme case, a child living in a Mumbai apartment house (or a city flat in Delhi or any large city). Here civilization is complex, artificial, largely hidden from view in its inner workings, and lacking appeal to the child's understanding or his natural feelings of cooperation and community of interest with his fellows. He cannot learn to take part in it by simple participation, except in its parasite activities, such as selling newspapers on the street. None of the necessary operations of obtaining food or clothing or shelter can be seen in their simple entirety. Food is something to be bought in a shop, often ready cooked: clothing mysteriously arrives finished and ready to wear: and father and mother certainly do not take any obvious part in preparing either. Although men in such a society are still more dependent on the cooperation of their fellows than in the pioneer community, the cooperation has become so complex that it is not seen or understood. The factory is a place with "no admission except on business" on its gates, in contrast with the mill, the wheelwright's shop, the potter's shed, or the tannery. There are few or no natural jobs which fall to the lot of the children and teach them to bear their share in the life around them; no chores such as splitting wood, or bringing in the cows, or helping in the dairy, or knitting the legs of the absolutely necessary stockings which cannot be bought but must be made. Artificial jobs about the home may be invented for such children by a mother who instinctively feels their wholesomeness, but they cannot be the natural tasks arising from the family life, and so do not carry with them the same training in character.

The school has a task it did not have before, the task

of supplying an environment which will approximate, in opportunities for character training, to what pioneer environment, a task which, if we value social solidarity and comprehending co-operation, we will rate as more important than its primary task of supplying letters. If this view is the true one, school should be a place where a natural communal life can be lived by the children, a life which will provide natural tasks to be performed, some individually and many in co-operation; which will supply problems to be solved, by action, not merely arithmetical or other problems in a book to be figured out, though figuring and reading will be found necessary and will therefore be learned willingly; and in which situations will occur where conflict can arise and the need of its solution be felt.

This principle is obviously similar to, indeed the same as, that preached by many German writers; for example, by Krieck, who extols the *Gemeinschaftsleben* of the progressive German schools. It goes farther than mere self-government in the usual sense, which is that a portion of the school discipline is handed over to committees of the pupils. It amalgamates the disciplinary side of school with the learning side, and the same problems upon which a group of children are engaged are at one and the same time the source of their book-education and of their training as citizens of their small community. To those who hold these doctrines, the division of the school time-table into artificial subjects is anathema; but so also is an organization like the Dalton Plan, where, although the time-table is wholly or partly abolished, yet the school-work is very definitely prescribed by authority, and is individual.

The basic idea at the core of this theory of the function of the school is that it must *be* a community, wherein those virtues only to be learned by taking part in an understandable communal life may be acquired. The school community, however, though simple, must not be stereotyped and delineated by authority. It must be a natural growth and progressive, so as to pass without break over into the growing and progressing life of the outer community of to-day, which no longer has such fixed forms as had the older type of society. Industry, trades, commerce, forms of government, have changed tremendously since our grandparents were children, and are likely to change more. The school, therefore, has lost the definite goals to which it might in an earlier century have looked, had universal state education then been introduced, the definite occupations to which its pupils might have looked forward, and the familiar forms of society and government which they could have anticipated. Instead, it has to prepare for an unknown future, wherein rapid change is certain, wherein trades will disappear and new occupations arise, forms of government will alter, and social conditions go into the melting-pot. It must train for adaptability.

In the past the school has not infrequently been used as the tool of some other institution, a church, a political party; has been employed to influence a national quarrel or a racial tug-of-war. What is to be our attitude towards any such claims, or the danger of such influences, to-day? The problem is so thorny that many take refuge in restricting the school to that narrow function of giving literacy which we have admitted to be its original and peculiar task. As far as religion is concerned, America has banned it entirely from her state schools, and left it to the churches: and if a denomination believes that the religious teaching it considers necessary can only be given in a full-time day-school with the desired religious atmosphere at all times and in all lessons, then such a denomination in America must pay entirely for the school it wants, though it is permitted to have it if willing to pay. England (and Wales), in the "provided" state schools, has an hour set apart for religious teaching, but stipulates that this must not reflect the particular doctrines of any sect, but only give teaching in the tenets of the Christian faith common to all Christians, from the Bible; and, moreover, the parents may withdraw the children during that hour for instruction elsewhere. In the "non-provided" schools teaching in the doctrine of the church providing the building is given. The church in question pays for repairs and extensions, and has a veto on the appointments to the teaching staff, but the running costs are borne by the state. In Scotland practically all schools are either Presbyterian or Roman Catholic, are built by the state or bought from the church, are run by public money, and staffed by teachers of the same faith as is officially taught in the school. In Germany most schools are of a particular denomination, usually Lutheran or Roman Catholic, even though state supported; but some schools which have children of both religions have a proportional number of teachers of these religions, and re-classify their pupils for the hour of religious instruction. The *Weltliche* schools are anti-religious, Marxian in philosophy, and only found in the communist quarters of great cities. It is hard to find any principle to which to hold fast in such a difficult question. Religious toleration and freedom to worship as conscience dictates are agreed to, at least outwardly, by all. Few, however, push this to the length of avoiding an appearance of influencing children towards the religion they themselves follow, and most would consider such an extreme form of "toleration" as sheer wickedness, and leaving to chance influences what ought to be the most painful care of the older generation in its influence on the younger. For good or for ill, however, the state school of most European and American countries nowadays leave this matter very much to one side, either explicitly and avowedly or practically, and it is certain that if state schools, even in those countries which permit and encourage the teaching of religious doctrines, were to be employed very actively in the propagation of that religion, especially in the conversion of the children of those of other sects, there would be a strong public movement against them. The general principle seems to be, that anyone may worship as he likes, and may do what he likes, individually or in concert with his fellow-religionists, to bring up his own children in that faith, short of interfering with the liberty of others. If his faith is that this can only be done in combination with the whole education of the children in their ordinary schools, then the states in various ways have shown themselves willing to co-operate with him, closely in Scotland and Germany, indirectly in England, and only by permitting him to contract out altogether in America. No country has to our knowledge enforced a law compelling all children to attend a state non-religious school. Germany has passed and is enforcing a law to compel all without exception to attend state schools, but these teach religion. America has excluded religion from the state schools, but still permits "parochial" schools to take their place. We do not speak of France, of which we know too little, or of Italy, where recent changes have reintroduced religion into state schools, though in ways of which it is still too early to foresee the effect.

Other questions of belief are only a step less difficult of treatment in the school, especially the state school. National pride and patriotism, for example, is, in its purest form, a worthy sentiment, and one without which a boy or girl could hardly rise to still higher ideals. But, quite apart from the obvious danger that pride in one's own country may pass over into contempt and enmity for another, there is the difficulty that within one's own country different parties have different ideas of what we ought to be proud of. America has had to teach American patriotism more obviously than other countries because of her immigration problem. There, Old Glory stands on every school platform, and hangs in most classrooms. We do not display the British Union Jack in the same way, and if we had, we fear that in some recent years it might have led to friction, as even the observance of Empire Day has. It seems that in these matters of sentiment, and certainly in matters of party politics, a principle not unlike that ruling in respect of religion has to be observed, and controversial matters kept out of the schools, or admitted only under strict safeguards. All this means that, while the function of the school has been widened by the progress and complexity of our civilization, it has also in other directions been narrowed, chiefly because it has become a state school and therefore very sensitive to the sentiments of conflicting bodies of thought in its public. It has to train character in a way not necessary in the primitive community, as Dewey asserts. But it must do so without much reference to religion, and without any to party politics, which are coming more and more to include sociological questions of the very essence of the problems the school as a microcosm of the outer world must itself experience. America has a less problem in the political sense, since it practically has no party politics in the Englishman's understanding of those words. No Englishman could ever distinguish between Republicans and Democrats except by means of a mnemonic, and exponents of a more radical type of thought do not appear to exist in sufficient numbers thereto "cut any ice".

Perchance there are some forms of propaganda against which few, if any, have a word to say: for example, propaganda in favour of health and sanitation. That this is necessary and permitted is directly a result of our civilization, which has brought larger numbers than ever before into cities and under the influence of unnatural conditions of life even in the country, and indirectly a result of that civilization, which has undoubtedly made us all more sensitive to these problems. The growth and influence of the school medical service is one of the wonderful features of educational history in the twentieth century. The spokesmen of the medical profession want more treatment, and less mere inspection, to form part of that service, especially preventive treatment. They are anxious that there should be more direct teaching of hygiene and sanitation in the schools by the regular teachers, and they approve of the teaching of cookery, homemaking, and nursing to girls before they leave school, since in very few years many of them will become the mothers of a new generation of school-children.

Apart from this matter of sanitation, in all the newer ways in which the school is desired by progressive educationists to function, it seems as though the van is going to be led by the babies. It has been a commonplace for a quarter of a century that the infant schools were the best schools. We will not venture to guess why, whether because of Froebel's, and, later, Montessori's influence; or because in them woman has almost a free hand, while other schools are man-made; or merely because the shadow of examinations is still far distant, and the teachers can educate without doing it to order. Anyhow, even the infant schools are now superseded in progressiveness by the nursery schools, which care for toddlers between two and five. Their aim, in the words of Dame Margaret McMillan, is "to supply a nature day of nine hours", during which the toddlers form a community in which cleanliness, fresh air, and good habits rule; in which the behaviour needed in a community is learned by doing; in which freedom of individual action is never repressed, and is unchecked except by the harmony of the community.

NOTES

1. Especially by Washburne of Winnetka; and also in Germany. For example, in *Die Lehrerfrage in der neuen Schule* (Weimar, 1927), Vladimir Spasitsch says: "The instruction in the *Lebensgemeinschaftschule* is often divided, especially for the older classes into *Kern-* and *Kursunterricht*, essentials and courses. In the *Kernunterricht* those matters and those techniques are handled which all children must master. *Kernunterricht* is, therefore, obligatory for all. In the *Kursunlericht* those materials and techniques are handled which serve to discover and develop the special qualities and powers, interests and gifts of the children, and hence such courses are for the most part elective."

2. Pestalozzi makes Gertrud say: "You should do for the children what their parents fail to do for them".

6

Education at the Crossroads

The Education of Man

The general title I have chosen is *Education at the Crossroads*. I might also have entitled these chapters *The Education of Man*, though such a title may unintentionally seem provocative: for many of our contemporaries know primitive man, or Western man, or the man of the Renaissance, or the man of the industrial era, or the criminal man, or the bourgeois man, or the working man, but they wonder what is meant when we speak of man.

Of course the job of education is not to shape the Platonist man-in-himself, but to shape a particular child belonging to a given nation, a given social environment, a given historical age. Yet before being a child of the twentieth century, an American-born or European-born child, a gifted or a retarded child, this child is a child of man. Before being a civilized man—at least I hope I am—and a Frenchman nurtured in Parisian intellectual circles, I am a man. If it is true, moreover, that our chief duty consists, according to the profound saying of the Greek poet, Pindar, in *becoming who we are*, nothing is more important for each of us, or more difficult, than *to become a man*. Thus the chief task of education is above all to shape man, or to guide the evolving dynamism through which man forms himself as a man. That is why I might have taken for my title *The Education of Man*.

**Note*: This article is drawn from the writings of Jacques Maritain.

We shall not forget that the word education has a triple yet intermingled connotation, and refers either to any process whatsoever by means of which man is shaped and led toward fulfilment (education in its broadest sense), or to the task of formation which adults intentionally undertake with regard to youth, or, in its strictest sense, to the special task of schools and universities.

In the present chapter I shall discuss the aims of education. In the course of this discussion we are to meet and examine, by the way, some significant misconceptions regarding education—seven of them in all.

Man is not merely an animal of nature, like a skylark or a bear. He is also an animal of culture, whose race can subsist only within the development of society and civilization, he is a *historical* animal: hence the multiplicity of cultural or ethico-historical patterns into which man is diversified; hence, too the essential importance of education. Due to the very fact that he is endowed with a knowing power which is unlimited and which nonetheless only advances step by step, man cannot progress in his own specific life, both intellectually and morally, without being helped by collective experience previously accumulated and preserved, and by a regular transmission of acquired knowledge. In order to reach self-determination for which he is made, he needs discipline and tradition, which will both weigh heavily on him and strengthen him so as to enable him to struggle against them—which will enrich that very tradition—and the enriched tradition will make possible new struggles, and so forth.

The First Misconception: A Disregard of Ends

Education is an art, and an especially difficult one. Yet it belongs by its nature to the sphere of ethics and practical wisdom. Education is an *ethical* art (or rather a practical wisdom in which a determinate art is embodied). Now every art is a dynamic trend toward an object to be achieved, which is the aim of this art. There is no art without ends, art's very vitality is the energy with which it tends toward its end, without stopping at any intermediary step.

Here we see from the outset the two most general misconceptions against which education must guard itself. The first misconception is a lack or disregard of ends. If means are liked and cultivated for the sake of their own perfection, and not as means alone, to that very extent they cease to lead to the end, and art loses its practicality; its vital efficiency is replaced by a process of infinite multiplication, each means developing and spreading for its own sake. This supremacy of means over end and the consequent collapse of all sure purpose and real efficiency seem to be the main reproach to contemporary education. The means are not bad. On the contrary, they are generally much better than those of the old pedagogy. The misfortune is precisely that they are so good that we lose sight of the end. Hence the surprising weakness of education today, which proceeds from our attachment to the very perfection of our modern educational means and methods and our failure to bend them toward the end. The child is so well tested and observed, his needs so well detailed, his psychology so clearly cut out, the methods for making its easy for him everywhere so perfected, that the end of all these commendable improvements runs the risk of being forgotten or disregarded. Thus modern medicine is often hampered by the very excellence of its means: for instance, when a doctor makes the examination of the patient's reactions so perfectly and carefully in his laboratory that he forgets the cure; in the meantime the patient may die, for having been too well tended, or rather analyzed. The scientific improvement of the pedagogical means and methods is in itself outstanding progress. But the more it takes on importance, the more it requires a parallel strengthening of practical wisdom and of the dynamic trend toward the goal.

The Second Misconception: False Ideas Concerning the End

The second general error or misconception of education

does not consist of an actual dearth of appreciation of the end but false or incomplete ideas concerning the nature of this end. The educational task is both greater and more mysterious and, in a sense, humbler than many imagine. If the aim of education is the helping and guiding of man toward his own human achievement, education canot escape the problems and entanglements of philosophy, for it supposes by its very nature a philosophy of man, and from the outset it is obliged to answer the question: "What is man?" which the philosophical sphnix is asking.

The Scientific and the Philosophical-Religious Idea of Man

I should like to observe at this point that, definitely speaking, there are only two classes or categories of notions concerning man which play fair, so to speak: the purely scientific idea of man and the philosophical-religious one. According to its genuine methodological type, the scientific idea of man, like every idea recast by strictly experimental science, gets rid as far as possible of any ontological content, so that it may be entirely verifiable in sense-experience. On this point the most recent theorists of science, the neopositivists of the school of Vienna, are quite right. The purely scientific idea of man tends only to link together measurable and observable data taken as such, and is determined from the very start not to consider anything like being or essence, not to answer any question like: Is there a soul or isn't there? Does the spirit exist or only matter? Is there freedom or determinism? Purpose or chance? Value or simple fact? For such questions are out of the realm of science. The purely scientific idea of man is, and must be, a phenomenalized idea without reference to ultimate reality.

The philosophical-religious idea of man, on the contrary, is an ontological idea. It is not entirely verifiable in sense-experience, though it possesses criteria and proofs of its own, and it deals with the essential and intrinsic, though not visible or tangible characters, and with the intelligible density of that being which we call man.

Now it is obvious that the purely scientific idea of man can provide us with invaluable and ever-growing information concerning the means and tools of education, but by itself it can neither primarily found nor primarily guide education, for education needs primarily to know what man *is*, what is the nature of man and the scale of values it essentially involves; and the purely scientific idea of man, because it ignores "being-as-such," does not know such things, but only what emerges from the human being in the realm of sense observation and measurement. Young Tom, Dick or Harry, who are the subjects of education, are not only a set of physical, biological, and psychological phenomena, the knowledge of which is moreover thoroughly needed and necessary; they are the children of man—this very name "man" designating for the common sense of parents, educators, and society the same ontological mystery as is recognized in the rational knowledge of philosophers and theologians.

It should be pointed out that if we tried to build education on the single pattern of the scientific idea of man and carry it out accordingly, we could only do so by distorting or warping this idea: for we should have to ask what is the nature and density of man, and we should be pressing the only idea at our disposal, that is the scientific one, for an answer to our question. Then we would try, contrary to its type, to draw from it a kind of metaphysics. From the logical point of view, we would have a spurious metaphysics disguised as science and yet deprived of any really philosophical insight; and from the practical point of view, we would have a denial or misconception of those very realities and values without which education loses all human sense or becomes the training of an animal for the utility of the state.

Thus the fact remains that the complete and integral idea of man which is the prerequisite of education can only be a philosophical and religious idea of man. I say philosophical, because this idea pertains to the nature or essence of man; I say religious, because of the existential status of this human nature in relation to God and the special gifts and trials and vocation involved.

The Christian Idea of Man

There are many forms of the philosophical and religious idea of man. When I state that the education of man, in order to completely well grounded, must be based upon the Christian idea of man, it is because I think that this idea of man is the true one, not because I see our civilization actually permeated with this idea. Yet, for all that, the man of our civilization *is* the Christian man, more or less secularized. Consequently we may accept this idea as a common basis and imply that it is to be agreed upon by the common consciousness in our civilized countries, except among those who adhere to utterly opposite outlooks, like materialistic metaphysics, positivism, or skepticism—I am not speaking here of Fascist and racist creeds, which do not belong at all in the civilized world.

Now such a kind of agreement is all that any doctrine in moral philosophy can be expected to have, for none can pretend actually to obtain the literal universal assent of all minds—not because of any weakness in objective proof but because of the weakness inherent in human minds.

There does exist, indeed, among the diverse great metaphysical outlooks, if they recognize the dignity of the spirit, and among the diverse forms of christian creeds, or even of religious creeds in general, if they recognize the divine destiny of man, a community of analogy as concerns practical attitudes and the realm of action, which makes possible a genuine human cooperation. In a Judeo-Greco-Christian civilization like ours, this community of analogy, which extends from the most orthodox religious forms of thought to the mere humanistic ones, makes it possible for a Christian philosophy of education, if it is well founded and rationally developed, to play an inspiring part in the concert, even for those who do not share in the creed of its supporters. Be it added, by the way, that the term concert, which I just used, seems rather euphemistic with regard to our "modern philosophies of education," whose discordant voices have been so valuably studied in Professor Brubacher's book.[1]

In answer to our question, then, "What is man?" we may give the Greek, Jewish, and Christian idea of man: man as an animal endowed with reason, whose supreme dignity is in the intellect; and man as a free individual in personal relation with God, whose supreme righteousness consists in voluntarily obeying the law of God; and man as a sinful and wounded creature called to divine life and to the freedom of grace, whose supreme perfection consists of love.

Human Personality

From the philosophical point of view alone the main concept to be stessed here is the concept of human personality. Man is a person, who holds himself in hand by his intelligence and his will. He does not merely exist as a physical being. There is in him a richer and nobler existence; he has spiritual superexistence through knowledge and love. He is thus, in some way, a whole, not merely a part; he is a universe unto himself, a microcosm in which the great universe in its entirety can be encompassed through knowledge. And through love he can give himself freely to beings who are to him, as it were, other selves; and for this relationship no equivalent can be found in the physical world.

If we seek the prime root of all this, we are led to the acknowledgement of the full philosophical reality of that concept of the soul, so variegated in its connotations, which Aristotle described as the first principle of life in any organism and viewed as endowed with supramaterial intellect in man, and which Christianity revealed as the dwelling place of God and as made for eternal life. In the flesh and bones of man there exists a soul which is a spirit and which has a greater value than the whole physical universe. Dependent though he may be upon the slightest accidents of matter, the human person exists by virtue of the existence of his soul, which dominates time and death. It is the spirit which is the root of personality.

The notion of personality thus involves that of wholeness and independence. To say that a man is a person is to say that in the depth of his being he is more a whole than a part and more independent than servile. It is this mystery of our nature which religious thought designates when it says that the person is the image of God. A person possess absolute dignity because he is in direct relationship with the realm of being, truth, goodness, and beauty, and with God, and it is only with these that he can arrive at his complete fulfilment. His spiritual fatherland consists of the entire order of things which have absolute value, and which reflect, in some manner, a divine Absolute superior to the world and which have a power of attraction toward this Absolute.

Personality and Individuality

Now it should be pointed out that personality is only one aspect or one pole of the human being. The other pole is—to speak the Aristotelian language—individuality, whose prime root is matter. The same man, the same entire man who is, in one sense, a person or a whole made independent by his spiritual soul, is also, in another sense, a material individual, a fragment of a species, a part of the physical universe, a single dot in the immense network of forces and influences, cosmic, ethnic, historic, whose laws we must obey. His very humanity is the humanity of an animal, living by sense and instinct as well as by reason. Thus man is "a horizon in which two worlds meet." Here we face that classical distinction between the *ego* and the *self* which both Hindu and Christian philosophies have emphasized, though with quite diverse connotations. I shall come back to this thought later on.

I should like to observe now that a kind of animal

training, which deals with psychophysical habits, conditioned reflexes, sense-memorization, etc., undoubtedly plays its part in education: it refers to material individuality, or to what is not specifically human in man. But education is not animal training. The education of man is a human awakening.

Thus what is of most importance in educators themselves is a respect for the soul as well as for the body of the child, the sense of his innermost essence and his internal resources, and a sort of sacred and loving attention to his mysterious identity, which is a hidden thing that no techniques can reach. And what matters most in the educational enterprise is a perpetual appeal to intelligence and free will in the young. Such an appeal, fittingly proportioned to age and circumstances, can and should begin with the first educational steps. Each field of training, each school activity—physical training as well as elementary reading or the rudiments of childhood etiquette and morals—can be intrinsically improved and can outstrip its own immediate practical value through being *humanized* in this way by understanding. Nothing should be required of the child without an explanation and without making sure that the child has understood.

Concerning the Aims of Education

We may now define in a more precise manner the aim of education. It is to guide man in the evolving dynamism through which he shapes himself as a human person—armed with knowledge, strength of judgment, and moral virtues—while at the same time conveying to him the spiritual heritage of the nation and the civilization in which he is involved, and preserving in this way the century-old achievements of generations. The utilitarian aspect of education—which enables the youth to get a job and make a living—must surely not be disregarded, for the children of man are not made for aristocratic leisure. But this practical aim is best provided by the general human capacities developed. And the ulterior specialized training which may be required must never imperil the essential aim of education. Now in order to get a complete idea of the aim of education, it is necessary to take into closer consideration the human person and his deep natural aspirations.

Conquest of Internal Freedom

The chief aspirations of a person are aspirations to freedom—we do not mean that freedom which is free will and which is a gift of nature in each of us, we mean that freedom which is spontaneity, expansion, or autonomy and which we have to gain through constant effort and struggle. And what is the more profound and essential form of such a desire? It is the desire for inner and spiritual freedom. In this sense Greek philosophy, especially Aristotle, spoke of the independence which is granted to men by intellect and wisdom as the perfection of the human being. And the Gospel was to lift up human perfection to a higher level—a truly divine one—by stating that it consists of the perfection of love and, as St. Paul put it, of the freedom of those who are moved by the divine spirit. In any case it is by the activities that the philosophers call "immanent"—because they perfect the very subject which exerts them, and are within it the supreme activities of internal achievement and superabundance—that the full freedom of independence is won. Thus the prime goal of education is the conquest of internal and spiritual freedom to be achieved by the individual person, or, in other words, his liberation through knowledge and wisdom, love and good will.

Here we must observe that the freedom of which we are speaking is not a mere unfolding of potentialities without any object to be grasped, or a mere movement for the sake of movement, without aim or objective to be attained. It is sheer nonsense to offer such a movement to man as constituting his glory. A movement without aim is just running around in circles and getting nowhere. The aim, here on earth, will always be grasped in a partial and imperfect manner, and in this sense, indeed, the movement is to be pursued without end. Yet the aim will somehow be grasped, even though partially. Moreover the spiritual activities of the human being are *intentional* activities, they tend by nature toward an object, an objective aim which will measure and rule them, not materially and by means of bondage, but spiritually and by means of liberty, for the object of knowledge or of love is internalized by the activity itself of the intelli-gence and the will, and becomes within them the very fire of their perfect spontaneity. Truth—which does not depend on us but on *what is*—truth is not a set of ready-made formulas to be passively recorded, so as to have the mind closed and enclosed by them. Truth is an infinite realm—as infinite as being—whose wholeness transcends infinitely our powers of perception, and each fragment of which must be grasped through vital and purified internal activity. This conquest of being, this progressive attainment of new truths, or the progressive realization of the ever-growing and ever-renewed significance of truths already attained, opens and enlarges our mind and life, and really situates them in freedom and autonomy. And speaking of will and love rather than knowledge, no one is freer, or more independent, than the one who gives himself for a cause or a real being worthy of the gift.

The Third Misconception: Pragmatism

Here we find ourselves confronted with the inappropriateness of the pragmatic overemphasis in education—a third error or misconception that we meet on our path. Many things are excellent in the emphasis on action and "praxis," for life consists of action. But action and praxis aim at an object, a determining end without which they lose direction and vitality. And life exists, too, for an end which makes it worthy of being lived. Contemplation and self-perfection, in which human life aspires to flower forth, escape the purview of the pragmatic mind.

It is an unfortunate mistake to define human thought as an organ of response to the actual stimuli and situations of the environment, that is to say, to define it in terms of animal knowledge and reaction, for such a definition exactly covers the way of "thinking" proper only to animals without reason. On the contrary, it is because every human idea, to have a meaning, must attain in some measure (be it even in the symbols of a mathematical interpretation of phenomena), what things *are* or consist of unto themselves; it is because human thought is an instrument or rather a vital energy of knowledge or spiritual intuition (I don't mean "knowledge about," I mean "knowledge into"); it is because thinking begins, not only with difficulties but with *insights*, and ends up in insights which are made true by rational proving of experimental verifying, not by pragmatic sanction, that human thought is able to illumine experience, to realize desires which are human because they are rooted in the prime desire for unlimited good, and to dominate, control, and refashion the world. At the beginning of human action, insofar as it is human, there is truth, grasped or believed to be grasped for the sake of truth. Without truth in truth, there is no human effectiveness. Such is, to my mind, the chief criticism to be made of the pragmatic and instrumentalist theory of knowledge.

In the field of education, this pragmatic theory of knowledge, passing from philosophy to upbringing, can hardly produce in the youth anything but a scholarly skepticism equipped with the best techniques of mental training and the best scientific methods, which will be unnaturally used against the very grain of intelligence, so as to cause minds to distrust the very idea of truth and wisdom, and to give up any hope of inner dynamic unity.[2] Moreover, by dint of insisting that in order to teach John mathematics it is more important to know John than to know mathematics—which is true enough in one sense—the teacher will so perfectly succeed in knowing John that John will never succeed in knowing mathematics. Modern pedagogy has made invaluable progress in stressing the necessity of carefully analyzing and fixing its gaze on the human subject. The wrong begins when *the object to be taught* and *the primacy of the object* are forgotten, and when the cult of the means—not to an end, but without an end—only ends up in a psychological worship of the subject.

The Social Potentialities of the Person

The second essential form of this desire is the desire for freedom externally manifested, and this freedom is linked to social life and lies at its very root. For society is "natural" to man in terms not only of animal or instinctive nature but of human nature, that is, of reason and freedom. If man is a naturally political animal, this is so in the sense that society, required by nature, is achieved through free consent, and because the human person demands the communications of social life through the openness and generosity proper to intelligence and love as well as through the needs of a human individual born naked and destitute. Thus it is that social life tends to emancipate man from the bodnage of material nature. It subordinates the individual to the common good, but always in order that the common good flow back upon the individuals, and that they enjoy that freedom of expansion or independence which is insured by the economic guarantees of labord and ownership, political rights, civil virtues, and the cultivation of the mind.

Consequently, it is obvious that man's education must be concerned with the social group and prepare him to play his part in it. Shaping man to lead a normal, useful and cooperative life in the community, or guiding the development of the human person in the social sphere, awakening and strengthening both his sense of freedom and his sense of obligation and responsibility, is an essential aim. But it is not the primary, it is the secondary essential aim. The ultimate end of education concerns the human person in his personal life and spiritual progress, not in his relationship to the social environment. Moreover, with regard to the secondary aim itself of which I am speaking, we must never forget that personal freedom itself is as the core of social life, and that a human society is veritably a group of human freedoms which accept obedience and self-sacrifice and a common law for the general welfare, in order to enable each of these freedoms to reach in everyone a truly human fulfilment. The man and the group are intermingled with each other and they surpass each other in different respects. Man finds himself by subordinating himself to the group, and the group attains its goal only by serving man and by realizing that man has secrets which escape the group and a vocation which is not included in the group.

The Fourth Misconception: Sociologism

Here we are confrontd with a fourth error of misconception akin to the third one, which derives the supreme rule and standard of education from social conditioning. The essence of education does not consist in adapting a potential citizen to the conditions and interactions of social life, but first in *making a man;* and by this very fact in preparing a citizen. Not only is it nonsense to oppose education for the person and education for the commonwealth, but the latter supposes the former as a pre-requisite, and in return the former is impossible without the latter, for one does not make a man except in the bosom of social ties where there is an awakening of civic understanding and civic virtues.

The old education is to be reproached for its abstract and bookish individualism. To have made education more experiential, closer to concrete life and permeated with social concerns from the very start is an achievement of which modern education is justly proud. Yet in order to reach completion such a necessary reform must understand, too, that to be a good citizen and a man of civilization what matters above all is the inner center, the living source of personal conscience in which originate idealism and generosity, the sense of law and the sense of friendship, respect for others, but at the same time deep-rooted independence with regard to common opinion. We must also understand that without abstract insight and intellectual enlightenment the more striking experiences are of no use to man, like beautiful colors in darkness; that the best way not to be bookish is to avoid textbooks as a plague, even textbooks in experientialism, but to read books. I mean to read them avidly; and to understand also that, in a more general way, the pursuit of concrete life becomes a decoy if it scatters the attention of man or child among practical trifles, psychotechnical recipes, and the infinity of utilitarian activities, while disregarding the genuine concrete life of the intellect and the soul. The sense of concrete reality is made blunt by utilitarianism; it develops and flowers forth through those activities which are all the more needed by human life since they are not at the service of any practical utility, because they are in themselves, freedom, fruit, and joy. Unfortunate is a youth who does not know the pleasure of the spirit and is not exalted in the joy of knowing and the joy of beauty, and enthusiasm for ideas, and quickening experience in the first love, delight and luxury of wisdom and poetry. Boredom and weariness with human affairs will come early enough indeed; to deal with them is the job of the grown-up.

To discuss the matter in a more specific manner, I should like to make the following observations: that conception which makes education itself a constantly renewed experiment, starting from the pupil's present purposes and developing in one way or another according to the success of his problem-solving activity with regard to these purposes and to new purposes arising from broadened experience in unforeseen directions, such a pragmatist conception has its own merits when it comes to the necessity of adapting educational methods to the natural interests of the pupil. But what are the standards for judging the purposes and values that successively emerging in the pupil's mind? if the teacher himself has no general aim, nor final values to which all this process is related; if education itself is to grow "in whatever direction a novelty emerging future renders most feasible";[3] in other words, if the pragmatist theory requires a perpetual experimental reconstruction of the ends of the educator himself (and not only of the experience of the pupil), then it teaches educational recipes but gets away from any real art of education: for an education which does not have any goal of its own and tends only to growth itself without "end beyond further growth"[4] is no more an art of architecture which would not have any idea of what is to be built, and would only tend to the growth of the construction in whatever direction a new addition of materials is feasible. In nature itself, biological growth is nothing but a morphological process, or the progressive acquisition of a definite form. And finally the pragmatist theory can only subordinate and enslave education to the trends which may develop in collective life and society, for in the last analysis the aims newly arising in such a "reconstruction of ends" will only be determined by the precarious factors of the environment to be controlled and the values made at each moment predominant by given social conditions or tendencies by the state.

The element of truth which must be preserved in the conception I have just discussed, is the fact that the final end of education—the fulfilment of man as a human person—is infinitely higher and broader than the aim of architectural art or even the aim of medical art, for it deals with our very freedom and spirit, whose boundless potentialities can be led to full human stature only by means of constant creative renewal. As a result, the vital spontaneity of the one to be educated plays a major part in the progress toward this final end, as well as the steady widening of the pupil's experience; and the need for constantly renewed adaptation of methods, means, and approaches is much greater in educational art than in any art dealing only with some material achievement.

The Fifth Misconception: Intellectualism

With regard to the powers of the human soul I should like now to indicate as briefly as possible two other errors which oppose one another and which come from overemphasis; intellectualism, the fifth error or misconception on our list; the other, voluntarism.

Intellectualism takes on two principal forms: a certain form of intellectualism seeks the supreme achievements of education in sheer dialectical or rhetorical skill—such was the case of classical pedagogy, especially in the bourgeois era, in which education was a privilege of privileged classes.

Another form of intellectualism, a modern one, gives up universal values and insists upon the working and experiential functions of intelligence. It seeks the supreme achievements of education in scientific and technical specialization. Now specialization is more and more needed by the technical organization of modern life, yet it should be compensated for by a more vigorous general training, especially during youth. If we remember that the animal is a specialist, and a perfect one, all of its knowing-power being fixed upon single task to be done, we ought to conclude that an educational program which would aim at forming specialists ever more perfect in ever more specialized fields, and unable to pass judgment on any matter that goes beyond their specialized competence, would lead indeed to a progressive animalization of the human mind and life. Finally, as the life of bees consists of producing honey, the real life of man would consist of producing in a perfectly pigeonholed manner economic values and scientific discoveries, while some cheap pleasure or social entertainment would occupy leisure time, and a vague religious feeling, without any content of thought and reality, would make existence a little less flat, perhaps a little more dramatic and stimulating, like a happy dream, the overwhelming cult of specialization dehumanizes man's life.

Fortunately, nowhere in the world has any educational system been set up solely on this basis. Yet there exists everywhere a trend toward such a conception of education, following a more or less conscious materialistic philosophy of life. This represents a great peril for the democracies, because the democratic ideal more than any other requires faith in and the development of spiritual energies—a field which is over and above any specialization—and because a complete division of the human mind and activities into specialized compartments would make impossible the very "government of the people, by the people, and for the people." How could the common man be capable to judging about the good of the people if he felt able to pass judgment only in the field of his own specialized vocational competence? Political activity and political judgment would become the exclusive job of specialized experts in the matter—a kind of state technocracy which does not open particularly felicitous perspectives either for the good of the people or for liberty. As for education—complemented by some imperative vocational guidance—it would become the regular process of differentiation of the bees in the human beehive. In reality, the democratic way of life demands primarily liberal education for all and a general humanistic development throughout society. Even as to industrial achievements, man's free ingenuity strengthened by an education which liberates and broadens the mind is of as great import as technical specialization, for out of these free resources of human intelligence there arises, in managers and workers, the power of adapting themselves to new circumstances and mastering them.

The Sixth Misconception: Voluntarism

Voluntarism, also has two principal forms. In reaction against the first form of intellectulism, a voluntarist trend, developed since the time of Schopenhauer, has contributed to upset the internal order of human nature, by making intelligence subservient to the will and by appealing to the virtue of irrational forces. Accordingly, education was intended to concentrate either on the will which was to be disciplined according to some national pattern or on the free expansion of nature and natural potentialities. The merit of the best and wisest forms of voluntarism in the educational field[5] has been to call attention again to the essential importance of the voluntary functions, disregarded by intellectualist pedagogy, and to the primacy of morality, virtue, and generosity in the upbringing of man. For the main point is surely to be a good man rather than to be learned man. As Rabelais put it, science without conscience is the ruin of the soul. Such was the ideal but in actual fact the pedagogic achievements of voluntarism have been strangely disappointing, at least from the point of view of the good. From the point of view of evil, they have had plenty of success—I mean in the effectiveness of Nazi training, schools, and youth organizations, in smashing all sense of truth in human minds and in perverting the very function of language and morally devastating the youth and making the intellect only an organ of the technical equipment of the state.

For the voluntarist trend in education combines very well with technical training. We find such a combination not only in the totalitarian corruption of education but elsewhere also, and there to some good purpose. As we see it in democratic countries, this peculiar form of educational voluntarism may be described as an effort to compensate for the inconveniences of the second form of intellectualism—overspecialized technical training—by what is known as education of will, education of feeling, formation of character, etc. Yet the misfortune is that this commendable effort has yielded, as a rule, the same disappointing result of which I spoke a moment ago.[6] Character is something easily warped or debased, difficult to shape. All the pedagogical hammering of nails into the shoe doesn't make the shoe more comfortable to the foot. The methods which change the school into a hospital for refitting and vitalizing the wills, suggesting altruistic behavior or infusing good citizenship, may be well conceived and psychologically suitable, but they are for the most part dishearteningly ineffective.

We believe that intelligence is in and by itself nobler than the will of man, for its activity is more immaterial and universal. But we believe also that, in regard to the things or the very objects on which this activity bears, it is better to will and love the good than simply to know it. Moreover, it is through man's will, when it is good, not through his intelligence, be it ever so perfect, that man is made good and right. A similar intermingling of roles is to be found in education, taken in its broadest sense. The upbringing of the human being must lead both intelligence and will toward achievement, and the shaping of the will is throughout more important to man that the shaping of the intellect. Yet, whereas the educational system of schools and colleges succeeds as a rule in equipping man's intellect for knowledge, it seems to be missing its main achievement, the equipping of man's will. What an infelicity!

The Paradoxes of Education

The Seventh Misconception: Everything Can be Learned

We are here confronted with some paradoxical aspects of education. The main paradox can be formulated as follows: what is most important in education is not the job of education, and still less that of learning. Here we face an error terribly current in the modern world—the seventh error or misconception on our list—which boils down to the belief that everything can be learned. Greek sophists, too, believed that everything, even virtue, could be gotten by means of learning and discussing the matter. It is not true that everything can be learned, and that youth must earnestly expect from colleges not only courses in cooking, housekeeping, nursing, advertising, cosmetology,[7] moneymaking, and getting married, but also—why not?—courses on the scientific means of acquiring creative genius in art of science, or of consoling those who weep, or of being a man of generosity.

The teaching of morality, with regard to its intellectual bases, should occupy a great place in school and college education. Yet that right appreciation of practical cases which the ancients called *prudentia*, and which is an inner vital power of judgment developed in the mind and backed up by well-directed will, cannot be replaced by any learning whatsoever. Nor can experience, which is an incommunicable fruit of suffering and memory, and through which the shaping of man is achieved, be taught by any school or any courses. There are courses in philosophy, but no courses in wisdom; wisdom is gained through spiritual experience, and as for practical wisdom, as Aristotle put it, the experience of old men is both as undemonstrable and illuminating as the first principles of understanding. Moreover, is there anything of greater import in the education of man than that which is of the greatest import for man and human life? For man and human life there is indeed nothing greater than intuition and love. Not every love is right, nor every intuition well directed or conceptualized, yet if either intuition or love exists in any hidden corner, life and the flame of life are there, and a bit of heaven in a promise. Yet neither intuition nor love is a matter of training and learning, they are gift and freedom. In spite of all that, education should be primarily concerned with them[8]... With regard to love, which is the soul of moral life, the whole problem of morality is involved, and I shall be able only to touch upon it occasionally.

The Educational and Extra-educational Spheres

Another paradox deals with what may be called the educational and extra-educational spheres. By educational spheres I mean those collective entities which have always been recognized as especially committed to educational training: namely the family, the school, the state, and the Church. Here the surprising thing is that on the one hand the family, which is the first and fundamental educational sphere, grounded in nature, performs its educational task while not infrequently making the child a victim of psychological traumatisms, or of the bad example, ignorance, or prejudice of the adult; and that on the other hand the school, whose special and vocational function is education, performs its educational task while not infrequently making the youth a victim of stupefying overwork or disintegrating chaotic specialization, and often extinguishing the fire of natural gifts and defrauding the thirst of natural intelligence by dint of pseudo-knowledge. The solution is surely not to get rid of the family or of the school, but to endeavor to make them more aware and more worthy of their call, to acknowledge not only the necessity of mutual help but also the inevitability of a reciprocal tension between the one and the other, and to recognize, too, that from the very start, I say from childhood on, man's condition is to suffer from and defend himself against the most worthy and indispensable supporters whom material nature has provided for his life, and thus to grow amidst and through conflict, if only energy, love, and good will quicken his heart.

Yet what is perhaps most paradoxical is that the extra-educational sphere—that is, the entire field of human activity, particularly everyday work and pain, hard experiences in friendship and love, social customs, law (which is a "pedagogue," according to St. Paul), the common wisdom embodied in the behavior of the people, the inspiring radiance of art and poetry, the penetrating influence of religious feasts and liturgy—all this extra-educational sphere exerts on man an action which is more important in the achievement of his education than education itself. Finally the all-important factor is a transcendent one, that call of the hero which Henri Bergson so insistently emphasized, and which passes through the whole structure of social habits and moral regulations as a vitalizing aspiration toward the infinite Love is the source of being. The saints and the martyrs are the true educators of mankind.

The Educational System with Regard to the Formation of the Will and the Dignity of the Intellect

We may now come back to the intermingling of intelligence and will of which I spoke earlier. We must here stress some characteristics of school and college education which are often insufficiently taken into account. School and college education is only a part of education. It pertains only to the beginnings and the completed *preparation* of the upbringing of man, and no illusion is more harmful than to try to push back into the microcosm of school education the entire process of shaping the human being, as if the system of schools and universities were a big factory through the back door of which the young child enters like a raw material, and from the front door of which the young in his brilliant twenties will go out as a successfully manufactured man. Our education goes on until our death. Further, even in this preparatory field, school education itself has only a partial task, and this task is primarily concerned with knowledge and intelligence.

Teaching's domain is the domain of truth—I mean speculative as well as practical truth. The only dominating influence in the school and the college must be that of truth, and of the intelligible realities whose illuminating power obtains by its own virtue, not by virtue of the human authority of the master's say-so, the assent of an "open mind," intending to pronounce one way or another "according to the worth of evidence." No doubt the child's "open mind" is still unarmed, and unable to judge "according to the worth of evidence"; the child must believe his teacher. But from the very start the teacher must respect in the child the dignity of the mind, must appeal to the child's power of understanding, and conceive of his own effort as preparing a human mind to think for itself. The one who does not yet know must believe a master, but only in order to know, and may be to reject at this very moment the opinions of the master; and he believes him provisionally, only because of the truth which the teacher is supposed to convey.

Thus it is chiefly through the instrumentality of intelligence and truth that the school and the college may affect the powers of desire, will, and love in the youth, and help him gain control of his tendential dynamism. Moral education plays an essential part in school and college education, and this part must be more and more emphasized. But it is essentially and above all by way of knowledge and teaching that school education must perform this moral task, that is to say, not by exercising and giving rectitude to the will—nor by merely illuminating and giving rectitude to speculative reason—but by illuminating and giving rectitude to practical reason. The forgetting of this distinction between *will* and *practical reason* explains the above mentioned failure of school pedagogy in its attempts to "educate the will."

Now as concerns the will itself, and the so-called "education of the will" or character-building (let us say, more accurately, with regard to the attainment of moral virtues and spiritual freedom), the specific task of school education amounts essentially to the two following points; first the teacher must be solidly instructed in and deeply aware of the psychology of the child, less in order to form the latter's will and feelings than in order to avoid deforming or wounding them by pedagogical blunders to which unfortunately adults seem naturally inclined (here all of the modern psychological research may afford great help). Second, school and school life have to do, in an especially important manner, with what I would suggest calling "premoral" training, a point which deals not with morality strictly speaking, but with the preparation and first tilling of the soil thereof.[9] Yet the main duty in the educational spheres of the school as well as of the state is not to shape the will and directly to develop moral virtues in the youth, but to enlighten and strengthen reason; so it is that an indirect influence is exerted on the will, by a sound equipment of knowledge and a sound development of the powers of thinking.

Thus the paradox of which I have spoken at such length comes to a solution: what is most important in the upbringing of man, that is, the uprightness of the will and the attainment of spiritual freedom, as well as the achievement of a sound relationship with society, is truly the main objective of education in its broadest sense. Concerning *direct* action on the will and the shaping of character, this objective chiefly depends on educational spheres other than school and college education—not to speak of the role which the extra-educational sphere plays in this matter. On the contrary concerning *indirect* action on the will and the character, school and college education provides a basis and necessary preparation for the main objective in question by concentrating on knowledge and the intellect, not on the will and direct moral training, and by keeping sight, above all, of the development and uprightness of speculative and practical reason. School and college education has indeed its own world, which essentially consists of the dignity and achievements of knowledge and the intellect, that is, of the human being's root faculty. And of this world itself that knowledge which is wisdom is the ultimate goal.

REFERENCES

1. Cf. John S. Brubacher, *Modern Philosophies of Education* (New York and London, 1939).
2. The "four cults"—skepticism, presentism, scientism, anti-intellectualism—listed by Dr. Hutchins (*Education for Freedom* [1943], pp. 35-36) are but offsprings of pragmatism's domination over education.
3. Brubacher, *op. cit.*, p. 329.
4. *Ibid.*
5. F.W. Forester and his work's influence has been great in many European pedagogical circles.
6. Voluntarism does not succeed in forming and strengthening the will, but it succeeds in deforming and weakening the intellect, by the very fact that it exaggerates the province of the will in thought itself, so as to make everything a matter of one's will to believe. It has been pointed out in this connection that "just as in the realm of politics, the primacy of will identifies authority with force, so in the realm of thought the primacy of will reduces everything to arbitrary opinions or academic conventions. There are no first truths, but only postulates, demands of the will that something be taken for granted. In some senses, all knowledge rests on acts of faith, though the only principle of such faith is one's private

predilections." Mortimer J. Adler, "Liberalism and Liberal Education." *The Educational Record,* July, 1939, pp. 435-436.

8. "I attacked vocationalism, and the University of California announced a course in cosmetology, saying The profession of beautician is the fastest growing in this state." Robert M. Hutchins, *Education for Freedom* (Louisiana State University Press, 1943), p. 19.

9. "Education ought to teach us how to be in love always and what to be in love with. The great things of history have been done by the great lovers, by the saints and men of science and artists; and the problem of civilization is to give every man a chance of being a saint, a man of science, or an artist. But this problem cannot be attempted, much less solved, unless men desire to be saints, men of science, and artists and if they are to desire that continuously and consciously, they must be taught what it means to be these things." Sir Arthur Clutton-Brock, *The Ultimate Belief* (New York, 1916), p. 123. Quoted by John U. Nef. *The United States and Civilization* (Chicago, 1942), p. 265.

9. The system of city schools as known in England and tried here and there in Europe has proved particularly fruitful for such premoral training.

7

Heredity and Education

To believe in the relative importance of heredity and environment will influence our action in segregating or otherwise the gifted or the dull, and in blaming or otherwise the teacher of a dull or a gifted class. Generally, if we believe more in heredity we will in our methods "keep the ring" and allow development, not imagining we are creating it. If we believe more in the influence of environment, we will expect good methods to show greater results.

Obviously, before we can come to any conclusions on this matter we must have at least a working knowledge of what is well established about the mechanism of heredity. The idea that like produces like must always have been familiar to man, for he could see with the most untrained eyes that an apple-tree did not produce figs, or the egg of an eagle a dove. Moreover, even in pre-Darwinian days the further idea, that within the species the children tended to resemble their parents in some detail, often arose, and Lamarck and others had theories of evolution based on this fact.

Darwin added an emphasis on the power of selection to modify a species by shortening the life and therefore the fecundity of some parents, and lengthening the life and therefore increasing the fecundity of others. Moreover, he widened the generalization to include the possibility of all genera as well as all species having been separated in this way from one common ancestor; and he did not hesitate to include man.

The changes since Darwin's time have been mainly two. In the first place, instead of the idea of selection working on infinitesimal variations, and by continued action over a long period of time producing any desired amount of change, there has come from the work of the Mendelians the idea of the variations upon which selection works being definite steps, units, or mutations, which may be large or small, but at least are not, as a rule, infinitesimal. And in the second place, the idea of the inheritance of acquired characteristics had until lately been fairly definitely given up, altahough the allied but easily distinguishable idea of the acquirement of heritable characters, the possibility of the environment influencing the germ cells, and hence the offspring, of an individual, has recently been placed on an experimental basis by the work of Harrison.

The Mendelian theory of inheritance is a theory which postulates that the nature of a certain quality in a plant or animal is settled by a minute "determiner" in both of the "gametes" whose union created the individual in question. The gametes are the minute sex cells, one from the male parent (the sperm, in an animal) and one from the female parent (the unfertilized egg). The individual developed from the fertilized egg has two sets of these factors, one set from each parent. For examaple, an edible pea plant has two factors which determine whether it will be tall or dwarf, one factor from each parent plant. If both the factors are factors for dwarfness, the plant will be a dwarf plant. If both are factors for tallness, the plant will be a tall plant. If one factor is for dwarfness and one for tallness, then the plant will be tall, tallness being, as we say, "dominant" over dwarfness, which is said to be "recessive". In the case of some qualities, however, there is no dominance, the result of two different factors being to give an intermediate or a different quality. For example, in a certain kind of fowl, mating white and black gives neither, but a new colour, which the fanciers call blue, produced when the fertilized egg has a black factor from the one parent and a white factor from the other. Dominance itself, according to a recent theory with statistical support enunciated by R.A. Fisher, is an effect of natural selection and one which curiously has nothing to do with the adaptation of the species to the conditions of its environment. But that is a side-track though it is interesting to learn that certain qualities dominant in one species are not so in quite closely allied species, and that changes can be expected in the degree of dominance, due no doubt to changes in the background of other qualities formed by the other factors of the make-up.

For each of his qualities, therefore, an individual has two factors, one from each parent, which may be the same or different. If they are the same the individual is "duplex" for that quality, or "homozygous"; if they are different he is "heterozygous", or "simplex", or "hybrid". The factors themselves are technically called "genes".

When the individual comes to form its own sperm or egg cells, however, each such gamete contains only one set of factors. The set of factors found in a gamete need not be the whole set which has come from the male parent, or from the female parent, of the individual who produces that gamete. Some of the factors or genes may have come from the mother, some from the father, of the individual who produces the sperm or egg. But in the sperm or egg there is only one set, and therefore the gamete cannot be hybrid.

These genes are borne upon certain thread-like bodies, microscopic in size, within the gamete, of which "chromosomes", as they are called, there may be only few, say four, as in Drosophila or the fruit-fly, or many, as twenty-four in man. In number, size, and form they are constant in a species.

With this theory we may try to follow the mode of inheritance of some simple character (such as tallness in the edible pea) which is dominant. Let us speak, however, of a hypothetical quality Q-ness. (1) Suppose we mate two individuals who are pure-bred for Q-ness. That is to say, they are duplex for that quality, and have each the double factor. All the gametes of both these individuals, therefore, will carry a Q-ness gene, and the union of two such gametes will necessarily give rise to a duplex individual pure-bed for Q-ness (Case 1).

Case 1. qq mates with qq. Children qq, qq, qq, qq.

(2) Still more easily we can see that if each parent is "nulliplex" for Q-ness—that is, if neither gene of either parent is a Q-gene—then none of the offspring can possibly show the character (Case 2).

Case 2. XX mates with xx. Children xx, xx, xx, xx.

(3) Let us now, however, mate two individuals who are simplex for Q, are, in fact, hybrids. Each of the parents will exhibit the quality Q-ness in his or her own person, since we have postulated that Q-ness is a dominant character, i.e. one dose of Q-ness inan individual is enough to produce the external appearance of Q-ness. But since these individuals are simplex, the gametes which they produce will be of two kinds, one sort carrying a Q gene, the other sort carrying a non-Q gene. If a Q gene from one parent meets a Q gene from the other, the union will give rise to a new individual who is duplex, who will not only show Q-ness in his person, but will have two doses of it in his internal composition.

Case 3. qx mates with qx. Children qq, qx, xq, xx.

If a non-Q gene from one parent meets a non-Q gene from the other, the new individual thus formed will have no Q-ness in his make up, in spite of both is Q parents. If a Q gene from the male parent meets a non-Q gene from the female, or vice versa, we will have an individual formed who, like his parents, is simplex or hybrid. He will show Q-ness, but will be capable of producing gametes which are non-Q. The offspring of our parent couple, therefore, will be in the long run three-quarters Q in appearance (viz. qq, qx, and xq), and one-quarter non-Q (viz. the individual xx).

(4) In a similar fashion we can study the mating of a duplex with a simplex individual, where all the off-spring will show Q-ness.

Case 4. qq mates with qx. Children qq, qx, qq, qx.

(5) or the mating of a duplex with a nulliplex parent, where all the offspring will show Q-ness, but none of them can be duplex, all must be hybrid.

Case 5. qq mates with xx. Children qx, qx, qx, qx.

Note the peculiar fact that the offspring of two hybrids may be a pure-bred individual (see Case 3), whereas the offspring of a pure-bred duplex and a pure-bred nulliplex are all hybrid (see Case 5).

If the character attracting our attention had been a recessive character, the interpretation of these cases would have been different. Let us call the recessive character X-osity, and reconsider the cases with an eye on the character indicated by x. Since it is recessive, it will not show unless the individual receives two doses of it, one from each parent. In Case 3 only one of the offspring would show the character, which is not shown by either of his parents. In Case 5 none of the offspring show it, although the one parent does so. If, however, two of the offspring of Case 5 mate, Case 3 would be repeated, and we have the often-noticed phenomenon of a recessive character skipping a generation to appear in the grand-children.

These considerations make it clear that many persons may be "carriers" of recessive characters, and that we cannot find out whether they are hybrids or not, except by making them and noting the offspring. This is what leads to the prejudice against the marriage of cousins, for if there is any undesirable trait in a family which is of a recessive nature, it is clear that there is a danger that both the cousins, even though themselves free from external X-osity, may be carriers of it, in which case there would be one chance in four that their child would show the defect openly, namely if he happened to be the result of the union of a carrier gamete from each parent.

We are going over these facts not because the actual knowledge of them is of importance to educators, but because We are wish to convey the impression to those who have not made a study of genetics of the existence of a body of exact knowledge of the laws of inheritance which must have a very definite influence on our opinion of the relative importance of heredity and education.

The genes or determining factors are borne upon bodies called chromosomes, which are, as it were threads of beads, each bead a gene. There are in man twenty-four pairs of chromosomes. But we shall turn to the simpler case of the banana-fly, Drosophila, where there are four pairs. There are far more genes than four—several dozen have already been studied in Drosophila—and since there are only four chromosomes it is clear that the genes must be linked in four families, which tend to go together. We thus see that complications may arise in our schemes of heredity. Let us first of all consider the inheritance of two qualities on the supposition that the genes are borne upon separate chromosomes. Let us mate an individual duplex in both qualities with one nulliplex in both. To make for cleaness, let us speak of Drosophila and of the two qualities, long wings and greyness, whose opposites are stumpy wings and blackness. Then clearly every one of the offspring must have a long-winged gene and a stumpy-winged gene, and likewise a grey gene and a black gene. Since long wings and grey colour and dominant, they will all appear normal. Now mate one of them with a stumpy-winged black individual. Then, if the four genes of the one parent (long, stumpy, black, grey) were at liberty to combine at random with the four genes of the other, there would be four possible kinds of offspring: long-grey, stumpy-grey, long-black, and stumpy-black. This is not, however, what really happens, and the reason is that the gene for wingedness is borne upon the same chromosome as that for colour (black or grey), so that it proves impossible to separate long-wingedness from greyness by mating in this way.

Nevertheless, it does sometimes happen that qualities whose genes are borne on the same chromosome do separate in mating. This phenomenon comes about in this way. It will be remembered that each ordinary cell of an individual has two complete sets of chromosomes, one of which has come from one parent, and the other from the other. The gametes of an individual, however, i.e. the sperms or the eggs, have each only one set of chromosomes. During the process of production of a gamete the pairs of like chromosomes come together and cling and interwine intimately and closely. They then split apart again, and retire to different parts of the cell, which then divides in two in such a way that each half of the cell contains only one set of chromosomes. Now when a pair of chromosomes separate after having been intertwined, it seems that sometimes they swap small pieces of each other. In this way one chromosome may carry away some of the genes really belonging to the other, and vice versa, and so the intimate linkage of genes borne on the same chromosome may come to be broken.

It is clear that two genes are more likely to be separated in this way if their positions on the chromosome are far apart, like beads far apart on a string of beads. Whereas genes which are close neighbours on a chromosome will be separated much less frequently. This has enabled T.H. Morgan to make actual measurements, in units which have in honour of him been called "morgans", of the distance apart on each of the chromosomes of Drosophila, of the numerous genes which have been identified, a number now approaching one hundred. By the various permutations and combinations of these which can be produced by crossing, Morgan can produce at will many kinds of Drosophila. Some of the combinations, it should be added, are lethal, i.e. they cannot coexist in an individual which survives.

To complete an elementary picture of this Mendelian mechanism, we would ask you next to consider the phenomenon of sex-linkage in inheritance. Sex itself is a unit Mendelian factor of a peculiar sort, for the chromosome which carries the male quality is a kind of dummy; it may, indeed, be said to be missing. In Drosophila, then, a female has two sex chromosomes, a male has only one. Females produce eggs which have one sex chromosome each. Males produce sperm which have, half of them, one sex chromosome, and half of them none. The latter kind produce males, the former females.

Now Drosophila usually has red eyes. In Morgan's cultures, however, there appeared a male with white eyes. This white-eyed male was mated to an ordinary red-eyed female. They produced offspring half male and half female, but all red-eyed. If two of these offspring be then mated, one-quarter of their offspring—grandchildren of the original couple—are white-eyed; *and all these white-eyed individuals are males, like the original white-eyed insect.* The character is linked with sex. Let us follow this in terms of genes and chromosomes.

The original white-eyed male produces two kinds of sperm, with and without the sex chromosome. Those without the sex chromosome are in no way different from those (equally without the sex chromosome) produced by an ordinary red-eyed male. In neither case do they carry a sex chromosome, and therefore in neither case do they carry a gene for eye-colour, for this gene is borne by the sex chromosome. The "vacant" sperms (as we may call them) of our white-eyed male will produce, of course, males, and these males will all have their eye-colour determined by the mother; they will all be red-eyed, and will lack entirely the white factor.

The other sperms, however, will contains a sex chromosome, and this sex chromosome will carry the white factor. The females thus produced will necessarily be hybrids possessing both the red and the white factors. It is the red factor which shows in their case—that is to say, red is dominant to white. But their eggs will bear either the red or the white factor. When one of them mates with an ordinary male there are red and white eggs, and red and "vacanta" sperms. The files produced will, therefore, arise from the combinations:—

Egg.	*Sperm*	
red	red	red-eyed female
white	red	red-eyed female
red	vacant	red-eyed male
white	vacant	white-eyed male

The females, although all red, will not all bear the double dose of redness. If one bearing only the single dose is mated with the white-eyed male the possible combinations are:—

Egg.	*Sperm*	
red	white	red-eyed female
white	white	white-eyed female
red	vacant	red-eyed male
white	vacant	white-eyed male

White-eyed-ness will clearly be more frequent in males than in females. The reason is that it is recessive and cannot appear in a female, except when duplex. But a male only has the one chromosome, and therefore the one dose of white can be present without the counteracting dose of red, which would dominate.

The picture of heredity which is obtained by a combination of Darwin's principle of selection with Mendel's theory of unit characters is, therefore, one of a continual reshuffling of those characters by the mechanism of sex, which demands that a combination of genes from two individuals shall come together and form a new individual. This is as though each individual were formed like a new whist hand, by taking one-half from each of two existing hands. The pair of parent hands may be good, bad, or indifferent; they may have special peculiaraities, such as being suitable for a no-trump call, or a call in clubs only. The new individual, the new hand, may, however, be very different, for a new combination may arise which has very different powers from either of the parent hands.

Obviously, this process of shuffling and redealing unit characters which the sex mechanism provides will rapidly produce all sorts of permutations and combinations, and that these may be very numerous, as hands at bridge are very numerous and varied. When one remembers that man not only has twenty-four chromosomes, but has numerous genes on each chromosome, it will be easily appreciated that all sorts and conditions of men are readily producible by this means. On these permutations selection does it work, so that only some become the parents of the next generation. It will also, however, be easily appreciated that a recessive character will offer more resistance to breeding out in an unfavourable environment than will a dominant character, for a recessive character may be carried by people who do not show it, and who therefore do not suffer any selection on its account.

The theory, so far, offers no suggestion that anything new can occur except new combinations of existing factors. Before passing on from this to consider how new genes may perhaps be produced, let us remind ourselves that new combinations may be very new things in the most real sense. Plants produced by crossing may be most unlike the parents, and the bringing together into one individual of genes which have never coexisted before may well have most surprising results.

At the same time, most people feel a mental difficulty about understanding how the present complex fauna and flora of the world could have arisen merely from the various permutations of existing genes. That is why the inheritance of acquired characters is so natural a theory to think. Numerous experiments, however, have in most cases shown that habits or powers acquired by an individual during his or her lifetime are not passed on to the next generation by the mechanism of heredity, although they may be passed on by social inheritance, i.e. by education in the home or in the school. That is to say, the kind of life which an individual lives, although it may very profoundly change his own bodily or mental powers, does not, as a rule, change the kind of gametes which he can produce, and has no effect on his off-spring through heredity. This requires, in the case of the mother, to be tempered by the rememberance that during the parental stage of the child's existence the mother actually is the environment of the child, and so may have an influence in that way, although not through her gametes.

There have been experiments reported which appeared to be exceptions to the non-inheritance of acquired characteristics. One of these was due to a misunderstanding now cleared up. Pavlov's experiments on rats which were trained to come for food to the sound of a bell, and McDougall's experiments on rats escaping from a swimming-bath, are hardly yet, it would seem, to be regarded as confirmed. Recently, however, the work of J.W.H. Harrison has directed attention to the possibility of certain environmental factors influencing the gametes and thus creating new mutations. It had earlier been known that the *frequency* of occurrence of mutations in Drosophila could be influenced by external circumstances. Harrison had noticed that melanism was common in moths in industrial and smoky areas. Now, living in a smoky atmosphere makes a moth dingy, but doesn't make it black. These melanic moths, however, are quite black. Harrison took a colony of the normal-coloured non-melanic individuals from a distant rural area and divided them into two groups: a control group and an experimental. The control group was fed in the ordinary way. The other group had certain metallic salts sprayed on its food, salts which occur in the atmosphere of smoky industrial areas and are deposited on the leaves of the food plants of the moth. Those thus fed did not *turn* black. They did not *acquire* that character. But among their offspring, after a few generations, occurred one or two black mutations, a phenomenon which was absent in the control group. And the blackness thus produced was then found, on mating, to act as a simply Mendelian unit, usually recessive to the normal colouring. Harrison has since repeated and confirmed his experiments under different conditions, and if they are fully confirmed by others it would seem that we have here a case where we see an environmental condition modifying the gametes of an individual so that his offspring contain a mutation which neither he nor his ancestors have ever shown. Other species have been tried with similar results.

Harrison has also repeated and confirmed the work of Durken and of Brecher, who found that the pupae of a certain butterfly acquired under the influence of orange light a green colour, which was inherited, though it is not clear from the experiments *how* it was inherited. And in one case, that of an egg-laying instinct, Harrison claims to have given a direct demonstration of a true Lamarckian effect—that is to say, the inheritance of an acquired character in the ordinary sense. In any case, as he says, if the germ-plasm can be influenced in the way shown by his melanism experiments, the step to admitting the possibility of Lamarckism is slight. The situation, therefore, as to the influence of the environment on heredity is at present *sub judice*. But it still remains true that the majority of characteristics produced by education in man are very unlikely to have a "shock" influence on the germ plasm of the inheritance mechanism, such as may be guessed at in the above cases, and therefore for our purposes it is still true that most of our cherished qualities have to be produced by education afresh in each generation.

All these details will have given the impression that a great deal is known now about the mechanism of heredity, that those who are engaged on the work can to a surprising extent modify and change species by selective mating, and that environment, though its exact power is doubtful, appears to have extraordinarily little to do with the nature of the new individual, which to a far greater extent is determined by the genetic composition of his parents.

In various articles and books on heredity, human pedigrees can be found for a number of qualities, which look uncommonly like these Mendelian pedigrees. (e.g., in Crew's *Organic Inheritance in Man*, pp. 184 ff.) In some simple qualities, as eye-colour or certain malformations of the digits, Mendelian inheritance has been proved in man. In others, as in feeble-mindedness or albinism, it is strongly suspected, though the mechanisms are complex and perhaps several factors are involved. Davenport and others have also given pedigrees in which they have endeavoured to trace as unit characters such qualities as artistic genius, musical genius, or a proclivity for the sea. Such pedigrees are yet too dependent on subjective judgment in the decision whether or no an individual exhibits the character in question, and in any case such qualities seem unlikely to be units. Yet with little doubt but that in the course of time not only the physical but the mental qualities of man will be shown to be made up of a number of unit factors combined and linked in numerous but not untraceable fashions, and that we could if we wished breed different kinds of men as we have bred different kinds of dogs or of cattle.

8

Unity and Diversity in the Modern Intellectual Discipline

This essay will discuss the intellectual disciplines as one major aspect of contemporary culture. Roughly, we conceive their scope as comparable to that of the German term *Wissenschaft.* Perhaps their best criterion is general recognition in this country as main subjects for teaching and research in the central university faculties of Arts and Sciences. Thus, for most purposes, the "applied" fields that predominate in professional schools are excluded,[1] as are the creative and performing arts. Typically, the included disciplines are also organized in professional associations, both national and international, though the networks of such associations are extremely complex.

Here we will particularly address the problem of understanding the unity and diversity exhibited by these disciplines: the principles on which they are organized, the principles from which distinctions among them derive, and the principles they hold sufficiently in common that their common placement in typical "pure discipline" faculties is justified. That the intellectual disciplines can be treated as belonging together requires an explanation salient to problems of both the conjunction of cultural disciplines and the social organization of the university system. When, in so many respects, our society steadily becomes more specialized, why do our universities not specialize in one field, the humanities, the natural sciences, or the social sciences, leaving the other two for other universities? Why do such technical schools as the

Massachusetts Institute of Technology tend to "round out" by strengthening their humanities and social sciences instead of specializing in the natural sciences with increasing rigor? Similarly, the Brookings Institution, originally conceived as a graduate school of the social sciences, did not long survive on that specialized basis except as a research organization.

When conceived broadly enough, all the disciplines seem to share certain normative elements, that is, standards, or values and norms that derive from their common grounding in man's quest for knowledge. Whether the subject materials and natural phenomena, human behavior, or documents of the cultural heritage, in language or in stone, it is agreed that assertions about them should be solidly grounded in objective evidence accessible, if at all possible, to the relevant scholarly public. Similarly, inferences from factual statements should follow standard canons of logic, concepts should be precise and clear, and different statements claiming objective grounding should be logically consistent with each other. In social terms, scholars' assertions and evidence should be public and exposed to the criticism of professional peers. These standards apply no less to the humanistic disciplines than to the sciences. It is not necessarily required that a poet be logically consistent. But a scholarly critic of poetry must face the negative criticism of colleagues if his statements *about* his subject are not consistent.

These common standards of the intellectual disciplines, in which commitment to specific convictions other than procedural beliefs in their own importance and their own methodological standards is inherently tentative, suggest that a convenient distinction separates them from structures in which *commitment* takes precedence over further investigation, which necessarily places questions of how and why particular bases of commitment should be accepted above action on the bases of commitment.

Four basic areas of the latter type of commitment may be distinguished. Where empirical scientific knowledge is the primary focus, members of the applied professions must act with what knowledge is immediately available. Thus a surgeon responsible for a patient with cancer will operate to remove the malignant tissue to the best of his ability, ***not*** stopping for further investigation into the causes of even this particular cancer except insofar as he can improve his knowledge of the particular case within the available time. There seems to be a parallel line between humanistic scholarship and the "creative" arts. Like the good applied scientist, the good artist is certainly concerned with knowledge of the traditions and history of his art and with "theories" about it, but in the actual process of creation he is a practitioner, not an historical scholar or theorist. He must act upon his commitments and convictions, not primarily consider on what bases they are justified or not.

In the field of religious activity, the central concern is faith, which is a matter of commitment, not of posing a problem for investigation. The religious believer, including the clergyman, is not in the first instance a theologian or philosopher, but a practitioner, no matter how important the theological traditions of his faith may be. Finally, the distinction between investigator and practitioner has a speical application, which will be more fully discussed presently, to the relation between moral culture or "values" and social action. The responsible social activist, whether high official or ordinary citizen, defender of the *status quo* or revolutionist, is not as such a moral philosopher or social scientist, but once again a practitioner.

Contrary to much received opinion, I shall base my discussion on the fact that the proper classification of disciplines now seems to be broadly *tripartite* rather than dichotomous; we have the humanities, the natural sciences, and the social sciences. The last are the latest comers and are considerably more prominent in the United States than in Great Britain, or, indeed, France. The relatively late emergence of the social sciences as a "third force" seems to be a particularly important phenomenon—a deserving focus for the following discussion:

The Philosophical Background

The modern form of the intellectual disciplines originated during the Renaissance. In that early phase, they were, variously, *secular* studies not rigidly bound to *specific* religious premises like the theological-philosophical and literary-artistic endeavors of the Middle Ages. Stimulated by their encounter with texts long since lost to them, the humanists of the West eagerly undertook to recapture the civilization of the past, its religion, philosophy, art, science, even its social organization. Beyond this, it served as a point of departure not only for new and independent creation of their own in imitation of the ancients, but for such use of the riches of antiquity as Aquinas' theological appropriation of Aristotelian philosophy.

The humanities were thus the oldest and generally most prestigeful of the intellectual disciplines. With important components of theology, philosophy, and, eventually, mathematics, they comprised the core of higher learning throughout the Western world for a very long time, maintaining a virtual monopoly which was not really broken before the middle of the nineteenth century. They thereby constituted the principal common culture of the educated classes of Europe, with history, philosophy, langauge, and literature gradually assuming more prominent places within the same basic framework.

The natural sciences developed notably only in the late Renaissance, after the humanistic studies had been deeply absorbed. But despite the great achievements of such figures as Galileo and Newton—and the impact of their ideas on philosophy—the natural sciences did not effectually rival the humanities in higher education and the culture of the most influential social classes until well into the nineteenth century. Thus President Charles Eliot of Harvard, the most eminent modernizer of the American University system, was "only" a chemist, and his appointment was viewed very much askance because of the relatively low repute of scientists even at that late day.

It is often said that a most distinctive feature of modern Western philosophy has been its concern with the epistemological problem, the grounding of the validity of cognitive enterprises. The great seventeenth century synthesis certainly established a frame of reference that gave primacy to the problem in Descartes' sharp formulation of a subject-object dichotomy. This tended toward a metaphysical dualism of the knowing mind and the known external world.

Interestingly, such conceptions as Hobbes's "passions" and power or Locke's "sensations" and the association of ideas contained the germs of many outstanding later developments in psychology and the social science. Yet their prototype of the external world was the physical world as understood by the new physical science.[2] Thus, during its first stage, modern philosophy, as "philosophy of knowledge" concentrated on knowledge of the physical world. This comprised only part of philosophy, which was also concerned, above all, with metaphysics and its relation to theology. But with reference to empirical knowledge, the internal world of "experience," the subjective side of Descartes' dichotomy, was generally understood to be only a "position of the observer" for studying physical objects, not a category of objects for study.

It is curious—and would merit investigation in terms of the sociology and psychology of knowledge—that the priority given to knowledge of the physical world in the development of modern philosophy reverses the priorities applying to the development of the human individual's knowledge of his own environment and, it seems, the formation of empirical knowledge in early cultural evolution.

Since Freud, it has been known that the child's first structured orientation to his world occurs in the field of his *social* relationships. The "objects" involved in Freud's fundamental concept of object relations are "social" objects: persons in roles, particularly parents and the collectivities of which they are parts and into which the child is socialized. This orientation includes an empirical cognitive component which is the foundation on which a child builds his later capacity for the scientific understanding of the empirical world. What is often interpreted as the child's "magical" thinking about the physical world probably evidences a lack of capacity to differentiate between physical and social objects.[3]

Similar things appear true of cultural evolution more generally, though, coming under the general principle that ontogeny repeats phylogeny only very broadly: the parallels are far from exact. Perhaps the best single reference on the problem is the old article by Durkheim and Mauss on the forms of primitive classification.[4] This emphasizes, with special but not exclusive reference to the Australian aborigines, the priority of the social aspect of primitive categorization of the world, notably in the conception of spatial relations in terms of the arrangement of social units in the camp.

The Two Principal Conceptions of the Intellectual Disciplines

That these problems are crucial in an underlying sense is perhaps evidenced by the fact that the great British empiricist philosophers who most sharply crystallized the basic problems of epistemology were also greatly interested in human behavior and social phenomena—especially Hobbes and Locke in the seventeenth century and Hume in the eighteenth. Hume's essays, for example, contain outstanding insights into many fields of social analysis.[5]

This concern with both the physical and social worlds was the source of one of the most important movements from which modern social science has derived. It seems best to call the movement "utilitarian" in a sense close to Halevy's term, "philosophical radicalism,"[6] applying to the early nineteenth century. From it grew, first and perhaps with the most solid grounding, the main outline of the science of economics, in the line running from Locke to Adam Smith to Ricardo and his successors. It is no accident that economics could be relatively easily related to a viewpoint particularly concerned with the physical world. As a practical field economics is the sphere of social action most directly concerned with articulating the social and physical worlds, especially regarding technology's place in physical production and the psychological significance of physical goods in consumption contexts. The fact that money, the generalized medium of economic transaction, is quantified in a linear continuum having a logical pattern identical with that of the principal variables of classical mechanics is particularly significant in this connection.

Social science's other principal point of emergence from a utilitarian base was in psychology. Here the problem involved bridging the gap between concepts of the sheer givenness of the consumption wants of individuals, a cardinal reference point for economic theory, and the problem of explaining the genesis of wants or motives.[7] Insofar as handling this problem went beyond just postulating the association of inherently discrete elements (e.g. in the "association" psychology of James Mill), this frame of reference contained very strong pressures to "reduce" its psychological phenomena to more or less physical terms and lead directly into the heredity-environment dichotomy which came to dominate its biological thought. This has broadly produced the dichotomy between the "instinct" psychology of the Anglo-American tradition and "behaviorism." with its environmentalist emphasis and, hence, concern with the mechanism of learning. The crucial point for present purposes is that the differences between the social and physical aspects of the actor's environment were not considered problematical for the purpose of this type of psychology.

Like perhaps all great intellectual movements, utilitarianism had its "revolutionary underground" subverting the neat, orderly schemes of the main trend. The greatest of its representatives were probably Hobbes, one of its chief founders, and Malthus. Both were deeply concerned with the problem of the grounding of elementary social order, something which Locke took for granted.[8] The problems they posed were destined to play in various ways a critical part in breaking the closed system which gave the physical world, as conceived by early modern science, essential priority in the whole theory of possible empirical knowledge.

It will be remembered that this basically epistemological phase of modern philosophy took its departure from the Cartesian dichotomy of knowing subject and known object, and the attempt to relate them to each other. The empiricist-utilitarian phase of the movement seems to have retained a relatively simple version of this frame of reference, essentially treating its "subjective" side *only* as a point of reference and then concerning itself with objects treatable as involved only on the objective side. For the physical world this seemed quite appropriate, but it presented difficulties for the study of human behavior. It seems that the economists' insistence on the *givenness* of wants, involving *de facto* assumptions of their randomness, was in the first instance a way of avoiding the apparently hopeless complications of considering the knowing, wanting subject as also belonging to the objective category and requiring analysis on its merits. The complications derived from the fact that the Cartesian dichotomy had then to be conceived as being not singly but doubly salient. There were, concretely, no longer only knowing subjects on the one hand and known or observed objects on the other hand, but there were also entities in both positions at the same time. Insofar as they were both, how could specific structured properties of their different aspects relate to each other? It does not seem too harsh to say that the history of utilitarian thought has involved an elaborate evasion of this problem. The favourite device has been to hold, implicitly if not explicitly, that the subject-as-object in fact has no determinate structure. Insofar as it exists empirically at all, it consists only of given wants which, so far as they do not reflect physical realities, may safely be treated as random.

Kant, Hegel, and German Idealism

The alternative treatment of the problem was embarked upon, with all its enormous hazards, by the idealistic movement. The first step was taken by Kant. He focussed in the first instance on the skeptical consequences which Hume drew from the conception of an uncontrolled impact of sense impressions from all phases of the action situation impinging on a knowing subject as equally valid "experience." Kant's answer was that order could be grounded in the field of what he called empirical knowledge only by a sharp *restriction* of the conception of empirical knowledge to what he called the field of phenomena, which in effect meant the physical world in the sense of the relevance of Newtonian theory. This world could be ordered in terms of the combination of the forms of intuition, namely Euclidean space and linear time, and the categories of the Understanding—among which causality appeared with special prominence.

This realm constituted only a small part of the legitimate concerns of human interest. Kant, however, threw everything else into one basket. To the realm of phenomenal determinism, he contrasted the realm of freedom. To that of theoretical understanding, he contrasted that of *Practical* Reason. In this connection, one of his principal concerns was with the status of theology, which he radically denied could be a rational, theoretical discipline. Thus the realms of theoretical understanding and practical commitment were radically dissociated, the latter having radical precedence for all realms of human concern other than natural science.

Important as this was in setting the whole frame of reference for the modern intellectual world, it was very substantially modified in its subsequent development. The next major step was introduced by Kant's successor, Hegel, and consisted in a highly ambitious attempt to order the subjective side of the dichotomy in terms of the conception of *objectiver Geist*, or spirit, as it can sometimes be translated. The important concept here is in the objective element—i.e., that what are now often called cultural patterns, namely ideas, norms, or, more diffusely, "orientations," are treatable as *objects* of observation and rigorous analysis rather than merely as ways of locating the ultimate reference point for knowledge of phenomenal objects in Kant's sense.

Although he reintroduced the conception that the world of *Geist* belonged to that of objects. Hegel did not simply assimilate it to the physical world, but rather formulated its characteristics in a special way of the greatest importance for the future. "Ideal" objects were considered authentically objects, but they were to be treated conceptually in exclusively "historical" terms. The conception historical contained two primary components. One was that the historical object stood in a developmental sequence cognizance of which was essential to knowledge of it. The other asserted the object's uniqueness and, hence, in certain respects, its incomparability with other empirical entities.

Hegel himself built this into a grand scheme of the philosophy of history, interpreted as a process of the "unfolding" of the world spirit (*Weltgeist*) through the agency of human action. This had the greatest importance as one of the principal early versions of the general idea of evolution, antedating Darwin by nearly half a century. It also integrated the ideas of conflict and progress through the conception of the dialectic process in the famous formula of thesis-antithesis-synthesis.

Two themes involved in the aftermath, however, especially concern us. The first is the insistence that the field of human "subjective" concerns, of meanings, must be conceptualized in ideographic as distinguished from generalized and analytical terms. Secondly, the implications of the dissociation between the realms of the physical and of the "ideal" were pressed so radically that a certain duality of determinisms tended to emerge in the contention that each "realm" functioned according to its own unique necessities and in the failure to consider clearly how the "realms" interacted with each other. The dialectic conception of the ultimate unity of conflict and integration was a third major theme which, however, may be considerd secondary.

A complex set of variations on the theme of Cartesian dualism seems to have developed. We have not stressed the common philosophical concern with the difference between mind and matter, but rather the problems close to the issues of the development of social science. The social terms of the utilitarian tradition evidently emerged from what contrary to Kant's view, were the inherently open boundaries of the physical world as conceived by early modern science and philosophy. The utilitarian tendency was to assimilate analysis of human behavior as closely to that of physical objects as seemed feasible. The case of the logical structure of early economic theory is paradigmatic. The consequence was the extension into the behavioural realm of conceptions of the scientific treatment of a world of objects in a way which left the status of knowing subjects highly equivocal in this context.

The Kantian statement cut off this tendency to extension sharply. It radically shifted the problem to the field of the noumenal, which we can equate with essentially humanistic concerns, in German terminology, of *Geist*. Here the crucial questions concerned whether and in what sense the idea of science, conceived roughly as a compromise between the Western emphasis on physical science and the broader German conception of *Wissenschaft*, could find an application in the intellectual world of the idealistic movement. That it did so must be interpreted in terms of the operation of the imperatives of intellectual discipline, the general values of integrity in intellectual objectivity and generality, in the subject-matters of subjectively meaningful human concerns. Another process of "extension," parallel to the utilitarian extension of the paradigm of physical science, occurred here.

The sharpness of the Kantian dichotomy could not be expected to endure without modification. One reason lay in the fact that each of the two great traditions issued in an extremism having a profound bearing on the future structure of the intellectual disciplines. On the utilitarian side, it took the form of the pervasive physicalist reductionism that tended to hold that only the natural sciences, on the model of classical mechanics, could yield valid empirical knowledge in any sense. On the idealistic side, there was a corresponding radicalism that in a sense considered Hegel too "rationalistic" in attempting to formulate laws of the development of the *Weltgeist.* In the Germany of the later nineteenth century, Hegelianism thus gave way to radical "historicism," the conception of the universe as comprised of discrete, empirically observable "historical individuals" which were however, in principle incomparable. The sharpest formulation of the philosophical position of historicism in this sense was probably in the work of Wilhelm Dilthey.[9]

The emergence of this radically empirical trend was associated with a major intellectual movement in Germany, namely, the rise of the "historical schools" in a whole range of disciplines concerning human affairs, not only in history itself, but also in law, economics, and the cultural fields. This in turn involved a great deal of meticulous and detailed scholarship. The pull of this scholarship, as contrasted with the tendency to generalize, seems to have been responsible for a major division which appeared within this tradition and formed an exceedingly important background for the work, among others, of Max Weber.

This was the division between the atomistic and holistic trends within historicism. The first tended to break down the phenomena into minimum units and treat each as maximally independent of all others. The second tended to treat whole civilizations or epochs of history as unified entities. For the latter, the untranslatable German word *Gestalt* seems to be the best single characterization.

Very clearly, this entire mode of thinking tended to assimilate the whole sphere of human concerns to the model of humanities. Indeed, it carried this emphasis to an extreme comparable in certain respects to the extremism of physical reductionism. The attempt to relate the two main conceptions of knowledge to each other systematically was perhaps carried farthest by Heinrich Rickert, who discussed the basic distinction between the problems of knowledge in the natural sciences and those in the *Kulturwissenschaften.*[10] Contrary to the generalizing, analytical characteristics of conceptualization in the former, the latter were characterized by emphasizing the individuality of each phenomenon and therefore its inherent incomparability with others.

Movements Towards Synthesis

The two patterns of extremism, physical reductionism and historicist uniqueness and ultimate givenness, could not completely dominate the field for long, however prominently their theses still reverberate. Three main movements toward a synthesis soon appeared and have played an important part in the intellectual history of the last century.

The first of these can hardly be called a movement at all. Yet it has certainly contributed importantly to the present definition of the situation. On the Western, more "empiricist" side, it has involved a combination of biological and "humanistic" emphases. Its essential keynote is a concern with the phenomena of organization—and the fact that this emphasis directs attention to patterns of relationship rather than to units in the sense of the individual particle. The trend sketched above which united physics and classical economics generally gave primary consideration to units, that is, the wants of individuals were the particles of the economic system. Biology, however, with its concern for organization and structure, tends to emphasize "forms" or patterns, in the first instance as anatomical traits. Seen in this context, the emergence of Darwinism was a culmination rather than an origin—these emphases were "in the air."

From this viewpoint, "human biology," the concern with organizational traits, can move very readily from anatomy and physiology to the behavioural and cultural levels. Indeed, there is a long tradition connecting "natural history" with an historical approach to the study of human artifacts and "ways of doing things," viewed in terms of their meanings and functions, and social institutions.

This seems to be the origin of the predominantly Anglo-American discipline of Anthropology. Its self-definition, the "science of man," was conceived in a biological frame of reference as comparable to branches of biology, such as ornithology or ichthology, which studied other sectors of the organic world. In this respect, there was nothing unusual in the specialization on humanity, except that biologically it was very limited in time and variety, there being only one human species. Such study, however, inevitably led into the human traits which were separable from man's genetically organic constitution, which anthropologists have designated generically as his "culture." Anthropology then had to define its concern as the "environmental" side of the human equation, with reference to distinctively human behavioral phenomena, if "culture" could be considered to characterize these.

Within this definition, however, the anthropological concern was with "traits," not with particles. This was a radically different focus from that of the utilitarian economists, because traits were elements in the organization of human relationships, not properties of the individual human being. There was a much less direct correspondence with the logical structure of the physical theory of the day. In fact, the crucial point for present purposes is that this background of anthropology permitted a direct convergence with the trait particularism of the German historical tradition. This convergence was most directly mediated by Franz Boas, the most influential figure in American anthropology in the first part of this century. It is significant both that Boas was a biologist before becoming an anthropologist and that he was German. In the light of this connection, it is not surprising that anthropology also developed the alternative position within ideographic historicism in the idea of a total "culture" as a unified *Gestalt*. This occurred most prominently in the work of Ruth Benedict, whose book title, *Patterns of Culture*, gave a classic expression to this viewpoint.

The second, largely contemporaneous, though somewhat earlier, synthesis was developed by Karl Marx. It involved building a bridge between the pre-historical Hegelian works and the utilitarian aspect of the empiricist tradition.

All the emphasis in Marxian theory on "materialism" refers primarily to a contrast with "ideal" in the Hegelian sense, not to matter in the more primitive Cartesian sense. The theory does not seriously treat the physical world at all, and has had severe difficulties in the biological sphere. It is primarily an attempt to redress the imbalance created by Hegelianism in its idealistic emphasis by "setting Hegel on his head," as Marx said. The significant thing here is that Marx went rather directly to theory developed from a utilitarian base, namely, classical economics in a modified Ricardian form. As we have noted, this conceptual scheme had special connections with the physical sphere, but clearly was not itself a part of physical science—and it wholly bypassed the biological level.

The crucial Marxian concept here is "material interests." These are clearly economic in the utilitarian sense, which includes the assumption of the *unproblematical* character of individuals' wants. The concept attempts to introduce determinism into the system by postulating that, in the situation of the individual in a market economy, basically only *one* line of action is open.[11] For the "Capitalist" this is maximization of profit. For the "worker," it is staving off disaster by the acceptance of employment on the available terms.

Any serious student of modern industrial societies recognizes the tremendous oversimplification inherent in this scheme—no Western soceity has ever been that deterministic in precisely such narrow terms. Marx and, by and large, his followers have met this problem primarily by supplementing the economic element, which had the virtue of its special articulation with the physical sphere, with one which we could call political today. That is, Marx interpreted the structure of the situation in which interests in the economic sense were defined and pursued in terms of a socially structured conflict—which he construed as class conflict. This, however, involved the use of coercive sanctions by those occupying positions of superior power, the individual capitalist vis-a-vis his workers at the level of the firm, the capitalist class conceived as basically controlling the state at the macro-social level. The Hegelian dialectic of ideas was thus translated into a dialectic of interests which were both economic and political; the two categories were not clearly differentiated from each other.

It may be said that Marx took over Hegel's conception of the pattern of historical development, but replaced the *Weltgeist* with a modified version of Ricardo, and the periphery[12] of Ricardian theory in the broad utilitarian tradition. The content of this scheme was formulated in terms of human interests in "want-satisfacation" or goal-attainment, mainly at the individual level. But the paradigm of the Hegelian historical process, activated by dialectic conflict and moving through a series of stages, gave it a quite different meaning. This aspect is crucially significant because Marxian theory has never taken, with all its materialism, many steps toward giving human social behavior a generalized analytical treatment, but, on the basis of certain broad assumptions about "human nature," has relativized all problems to particular systems and historical stages of their development. For Marxians, Ricardian economic theory has been only the theory of capitalist economics and not an early stage of a general economic theory applicable, with others and with appropriate qualifications, to socialist societies.

Thus the Marxian synthesis, though certainly a genuine one, was incomplete in not breaking with the basic assumptions of the idealistic tradition in three respects. First, though it formulated, with heavy borrowing from utilitarian sources, the conception of material interests and gave it priority in analyzing the causal historical process, it remained historical in the ideographic sense and did not extend the conception of generalized analytical theory from the natural sphere to that of human behavior. In this respect it represents a retrogressive step relative to the great traditions of English economics from Ricardo through J.S. Mill and Marshall to Keynes.

Secondly, though repudiating the specifically Hegelian conception of the determination of human behaviour by the unfolding *Geist.* Marxism retained the "ideal"—"real" dichotomy of "factors," so that explanation was couched in either-or terms rather than terms of interdependence. The logical resemblance of this dilemma to that between heredity and environment in biology is too patent to need further discussion.

Third and most basically, Marxian theory, by accepting, largely implicitly, the utilitarian formula of the givenness of wants, tended to cut itself off from the most important problems leading toward a synthesis of the two sides of the Kantian dichotomy. The basic question is why, having freedom of choice, people in fact opt for one, not some other, personal goal and means of attaining it. The "ideal" component is postulated as given in Marxian theory, in a sense directly comparable to that in which the wants of individuals were assumed to be given in utilitarian theory. In other words, this is the area of an intellectual "neutrality pact," which in the nature of the subject-matter is suspect of inherent instability.

The period including the turn of the last century and the early decades of this century saw extraordinary ferment in all the fields of this discussion. A critically important development was the philosophical criticism of older views concerning the status of physical theory, strongly influenced by internal developments within physics itself. This was classically stated by Whitehead, who attributed a new level of abstraction to this type of theory, the ignoring of which involved the fallacy of misplaced concreteness.[13] This was clearly a more radical conception of the relativity of references to the physical world than that formulated by Kant. It demonstrated the validity of considering the same concrete empirical phenomena from the viewpoint of various different modes of cognitive interest, not just that of understanding in the Kantian sense.

A second major trend of the period developed interests in organizational conceptions in the biological sphere at the more physiological level, as well as at the more anatomical level. This extended the conception of organization involved in the original emergence of anthropology to dynamic levels. Perhaps the most eminent figure here is W.B. Cannon,[14] the physiologist. With *homeostasis*, he conceived of a spontaneous built-in control within the organism which maintained an equilibrium state within boundaries; this concept referred more to a "pattern of functioning" like that of behaviour than to an "inert" anatomical structure.

Still later, this trend of thinking established contact with that of cybernetics and information theory, which originated in the physical field of engineering more than in physics itself, but which has nevertheless grounded conceptions of an organized system maintained by integrative control mechanisms much more solidly in the *general* theory of science. This trend in the fields closest to the physical sciences has been most important to the development of a new status for the social disciplines. However, its primary references have been outside the latter field.

Another substantive field tending to bridge the traditional gap between the humanities and the natural sciences in a way directly involving the social sciences has been the science of linguistics. Language has been the citadel of humanistic studies. Indeed, German humanists in general have tended to call themselves "philologists." This is understandable, since language has been the primary medium of symbolic process and cultural communication. However, increasingly language has been subjected to analytical rather than merely historical study. Also, this trend has connected very directly with theoretical developments in the natural science field, notably information theory. Linguistics has also had important contact with the social sciences. First there was the older French work of de Saussure and Meillet. In American anthropology in particular, Edward Sapir and Benjamin Whorf have treated linguistic evidence as a main keynote of the idea of cultural relativity. More recently, Claude Levi-Strauss has been attempting to develop general social theory from linguistic models. It is perhaps not too much to say that linguistics is becoming a discipline that is concurrently a natural science, a branch of the humanities, and a social science.

A very significant methodological convergence should be added to these substantive convergences. First, logic itself is a general resource of all *intellectual disciplines*—as it has become refined technically, its general relevance has become increasingly evident. Secondly, logic has tended to merge increasingly with mathematics as a preeminent tool of analysis. Then statistics, from having been an empirical art, has increasingly gained mathematical foundations and extended its range of application, even into the humanistic disciplines, partaicularly via linguistic studies. The recent rapid development of computer techniques is a latest phase involving an application of a complex combination of these elements. The essential point is that these technical innovations cut clean across traditional divisions between disciplines. Their recent invasion of the humanities is the clearest sign that the latter cannot be regarded as inherently isolated from their "scientific" sister disciplines.

After this digression, however, we may return to the more specifically social and behavioral reference. Somewhat antedating most of the movements just sketched has been a third major synthetic development, following the anthropological and the Marxian. This, the emergence of the modern phase of sociological theory, may be considered synthesis of a higher order than either of the other two because it has included the principal components of the other syntheses and because it has avoided the extremism of the either or dichotomies which have plagued the other syntheses, namely, heredity-environment in the one case and ideal-material in the other.

Max Weber and Emile Durkheim

Two great figures were mainly responsible for this development namely Max Weber, starting in Germany from a critique of the idealist-historicist tradition, and Emile Durkheim, developing in France a corresponding critique of the utilitarian tradition.[15] These two converged very significantly on a common, though broad, conceptual scheme. Let us start with Weber.

Because of the relation to the humanistic tradition, it may be illuminating to note that Weber began his intellectual career in jurisprudence under the aegis of the historical school then dominant in Germany. This is significant because, in a very important sense, the law stands squarely between the two poles of the Hegelian-Marxian spectrum so far as human behaviour is concerned. Though, as noted above, legal norms, as rules and institutions, are essentially cultural in structure, they are relational patterns. As such, they are the first-line mechanisms regulating the pursuit of the type of interests which predominate in Marxian theory. Furthermore, so far as a society is concerned, law has a reference to the system as a whole, to the "public" interest, which is not shared with the "self-interest" of business of political "interest groups." It may also be noted that the Marxian attitude toward law has been exceedingly ambiguous. By grounding the conception of capitalistic interest in the concrete structure of the family firm, certain property institutions, and market structures regulated by institutions of contract. Marxians have generally tended to *include* basic legal institutions within the famous material factors, the relations of production. At other times, however, they have treated law as a component of the "superstructure," and thus as "determined by," rather than as a *part of*, the relations of production. The historicist pattern of thinking facilitates this ambiguity by denying the legitimacy of the abstract analytical procedures required to straighten out the problem.

From this juristic start, Weber embarked on an ambitious study of the "material" base underlying and interacting with legal institutions, mostly through various historical studies in economic organization after the genre of the historical school of economics of the time. He did so reacting against the "formalism" of much of the jurisprudence of the time, notably Rudolf Stammler's work. In his excursions into economic history, Weber did not, however, abandon the basic idea that legal norms *control* action in pursuit of interests, both economic and political.[16] Here he was very much concerned with Marxian ideas, but the retention of this fundamental position is a prime index of his refusal to become a Marxist.

A major reorientation in Weber's thought occurred after he had recovered from an incapacitating mental illness in about 1904, and was expressed in writings on a new front. Substantively the first important new work was the famous essay on the *Protestant Ethic and the Spirit of Capitalism*. This dealt directly with an "ideal factor" in reference to its significance for a specific process of historical development, indeed, the one Marxian theory had spotlighted. It was undoubtedly meant to challenge the Marxian view, but *not* in the sense of "setting Hegel back on his feet." Rather, it put the problem in a frame of reference neither Hegelian nor Marxian not historicist in Dilthey's sense.

The crucial point is that Weber's analysis, the core of which is the Protestant Ethic thesis, bridged the theoretical gap between "want" in the economic-psychological sense and "cultural patterns" in the idealistic senses. To put it simply and radically, Weber's solution was that, once cultural patterns of meaning have been internalized in the personality of an individual, they define the situation for the structuring of motives. Therefore, questions of how action makes sense must be answered by reference to the meaning-system defining the situation of action. Weber then postulated, not given wants, but given cultural definitions of the situation (the human condition) which make commitment to the satisfaction of certain classes of wants intelligible. These meaning-systems, however, were the very subject-matter of humanistic-cultural study.

Did this, however, constitute only a step along a line of regression which merely put the discreteness of cultural patterns, within which particular wants became meaningful, in the place of the givenness of discrete wants of individuals? At the very least, the discrimination of two levels in the want system, the concrete, satisfaction-oriented want itself and the cultural grounding of its meaning, would be a gain. But Weber's analysis went a step farther. He treated these as independently variable factors in the determination of action, which, in their mutual inter-relations and in relation to other factors, could be treated as interdependent in a system. This view basically broke through the ideal-material dichotomy of idealistic thinking about human action. The answer, analogous to that of modern biology regarding the heredity-environment problem, is that *both* sets of factors are crucial, standing in complex relations of interdependence with each other.

Before Weber, the "cement" which had been holding the parts of the dichotomy in their rigid relationship was the postulate of *historical* connection in its Hegelian-Marxian version. Thus, either the ideal constellation or that of material interests constituted a *Gestalt*, which either existed or did not, as a totality. A second focus of Weber's break with the tradition was salient there. He assumed as a matter of principle that the components of such a *Gestalt* should be treated as independently variable. He set out to analyze certain of these relations by the comparative method which in terms of the logic of science is the nearest empirical equivalent to the experimental method that is accessible to this subject-matter.

In treating the problem of Protestantism's role in the development of capitalism, any historicist, idealist, or Marxist would have treated the problems entirely as one of the sequences in Western history from the Reformation, and its immediate antecedents, to the Industrial Revolution. But Weber, in adopting the comparative method, studied the negative cases especially. Along with the question of why modern "capitalism" developed in Europe. Weber investigated its *non*-development in other advanced civilizations. He completed extensive monographs on China and India in this connection.[17] Again, the substantive question, how far he progressed toward the empiricial demonstration of his case, is not our concern here. The point is that his *method* involved an *analytical* isolation of classes of variables by comparing cases in which they demonstrably varied independently of each other.[18] In the subject matter of cultural* *Gestalten* this was a very new departure.

Concurrently, in a series of essays which, in the first instance, were polemically oriented, Weber attempted a principled grounding of this new orientation in the conception of empirical knowledge as such, but particularly in the context of the social sciences.[19] As noted he anticipated writers like Whitehead in establishing that analytical abstraction was essential even to physical science. By no means does its theory, for example, in the case of classical mechanics, simply "reflect" the reality of the external world. It is selective and hence in important degrees evaluative in its concern for empirical problems and facts. Thus it is partly determined by the interests and values of the scientist, among which possibilities of controlling natural events figure prominently, but by no means exclusively. This dependence on the evaluataive concerns of the investigator (which Weber called *Wertbeziehung*) had to be matched in whatever field, natural, social, or humanistic, by a favourable evaluative orientation to problems of the empirical disciplines centering about the canons of intellectual discipline, above all for objectivity in empirical observation and for logical, clear, and precise theoretical statement and inference. This is the focus of Weber's famaous doctrine of the "value-freedom" of social science (*Wertfreiheit*). It does not mean, as so many have erroneously believed, that the scientist or scholar should be free of *any* values, but rather that in his professional role, he must be free to give the discipline's values priority over others, notably in Weber's mind over political commitments. In contemporary terminology, I believe he meant that the values of the intellectual disciplines must be *differentiated* from other types of values constitutive of the culture. Only on such a basis can science and scholarship be institutionalized.

As a matter of course, however, Weber also insisted on the central importance of the "empathic" understanding (*Verstehen*) of motives and patterns of meaning as this had been emphasized in the humanistic and idealistic tradition, namely, the "subjective" side of the Cartesian dichotomy. These entities, however, were now also given the full status of objects, as regards both their own internal structure and the relevance to them of analytical abstracation and abstract generalized conceptualization. In certain sennses the utilitarians had prepared the way for this, but had shied away from its full consequences. They had preferred to limit this whole realm to the status of givenness under a set of restrictive assumptions, and to follow the problems of variability only in the other direction.

The *Verstehen* conception, however, was crucial to the new position because the impacat of the "ideal" factors as *variables* was to be systematically studied precisely in the definite, specific structures of cultural patterns, including legal norms, and motives. Both the utilitarian and the behavioristic positions simply foreclosed this possibility with bland philosophical assumptions.

On the background of these three essential doctrines of social science methodology, Weber thus culminated his argument by asserting that the social disciplines required generalized analytical concepts and propositions. Indeed, when Weber wrote, such theory-building had already advanced considerably in economics and parts of psychology. He, however, stated this requirement very sharply and clearly while discussing the idealist and humanistic tradition. Weber's own attempts at formulation in this field primarily took the form of ideal types. Though legitimate, they have certain limitations and constitute only one of a number of the necessary theoretical components of the social sciences.

Weber thus broke cleanly with the dogma that cultural and historical materials were subject only to ideographic conceptualization as forming unique historical individuals. His most important contention was that the more advanced analytical methods of the natural sciences must be adopted in the realm of the cultural disciplines—which meant primarily the humanities, but the bridge between the natural sciences and humanities was constituted by the new social disciplines. In Weber's case, above all, economics could not be allowed to remain caught between the imperatives of a "Western" analytical definition of its scope and a German "historical" one. Indeed, it can be said that the main rationale of Weber's venture into sociology was that he saw this as the only way out of the dilemma, the only path to a synthesis of the best in the two traditions of economics that could relate both to the essentials of the "cultural" sciences.

Weber's views in this respect cannot be said to have fully prevailed as yet. They do, however, constitute a break of such magnitude that a return to the positions of Hegel or Marx, or of Dilthey or Sombart on the idealistic side is clearly out of the question. Similarly, Weber's capacity to handle the relations between cultural movements and social organization in an historical and comparative context was such that a return to utilitarian modes of thought seems equally out of the question.

This conviction is strongly reinforced by Durkheim's striking convergence with Weber, even though they were of different nationality, did not communicate with each other, and knew little of each other's work. Significant to the convergence is the fact that Durkheim also was trained in jurisprudence. In his first major work, *De la division du travail social*[20] (1893), he used law as a principal index of the structure of societies.

Durkheim's critical point of departure was a devastating critique of the utilitarian position, couched in terms of Herbert Spencer's conception of "contractual relations," but covering the whole frame of reference back to Hobbes.[21] The crucial thesis was that, from a strictly utilitarian viewpoint, it was impossible to account for *order* in social systems, which Durkheim, using a Kantian pattern of analysis, treated as a *fact*, not a possibility. Paralleling Kant's famous question about empirical knowledge, Durkheim stated that social order, in the sense contrary to a Hobbesian state of nature, in fact exists. Given this fact, how is it possible?

Durkheim thus, from the other side, came to essentially the same basic conclusion as Weber. He established a connection between the wants of individuals, as conceived in the utilitarian tradition, and the normative patterning of the social structure, particularly as analyzed in law. The institution of contract was treated as analytically independent of the interests of contracting parties, but the former constituted an indispensable set of conditions for the effective satisfaction of the latter.

The basic theme of internalization of the normative patterns defining situations had, as noted, been partially worked out by Weber. It was considerably further analyzed by Durkheim in his studies of suicide and education—his famous concept of *anomie* was a name for the failure of this relation to become stabilized in the relation of a normative system to the personality of the indivual.

Conclusion

In outlining this intellectual history, I have attempted to trace a principal path by which the intellectual disciplines, institutionalized in the central faculties of American universities, acquired the foundation of a basic unity which is nevertheless compatible with their inherent diversity. In a sense it was natural that, as modern intellectual culture emerged, the humanities and sciences should hold radically different patterns of orientation, and that the social disciplines should be substantially less well crystallized.

The growth of knowledge itself, accompanied by generalization and sophistication on both sides, exerted pressure for firmer methodological and, eventually, philosophical groundings. Indeed, this pressure may well have been an important factor in the emphasis modern philosophy has placed on epistemological concerns.

In the movement emerging from philosophical empiricism, which included the physical sciences, utilitarianism, and eventually Darwinian biology, these problems were not generally brought into sharp focus. The social disciplines developed slowly on the basis of a rather empirical, common-sense view of the task of history, utilitarian theorizing in economics and psychology, and the extension of Darwinian biology into the behavioural fields.

This history clearly illustrates the difficulty of drawing

sharp boundaries to the domain of natural science within this frame of reference. One mode of extension into the social field, of which classical economics is the type case, could be stabilized only by a "walling off" against further extension by assuming the givenness of wants and their purely individual character. The development of biological thinking, however, presented still greater difficulties, since it introduced, particularly in its extension through anthropology to the human behavioural field, the especially important conceptions of organization and relational patterns. This, in its environmental reference, eventuated in the concept of culture, which on a utilitarian background, was a truly revolutionary concept. This too tended to be "walled off" through the trait atomist doctrine of the so-called "historical" school of British American anthropology.

The relevant intellectual history on the background of empiricism and utilitarianism involved a gradually increasing strain in the direction of giving a more independent status to the human cultural-behavioural fields, but attended by a continuing anxiety that doing so would imply abandoning the attempt to be scientific. Kant introduced a clean break in these respects, explicitly confining science to the field of physical phenomena—only this limited area was accessible to the methods of "pure reason." Problems of how the areas of human behaviour excluded from science could be treated as objects of observation and analysis thereby became acute. The idealistic movement, especially with Hegel, solved this by focusing on the conception of *Geist* as itself objectively observavabale through a rather different kind of "understanding" than the Kantian, namely, that conveyed by later uses of the German term *Verstehen*. The problem here was the obverse of the one posed for the utilitarian tradition, namely, not how to treat human motives or wants as independent of their conditioning substratum in the physical world or the organism, but how to relate the imperatives of ideal patterns to the exigencies of the real world in a way accounting for the realistically effective qualities of such entities in actual behaviour. This orientation went through two stages: the Hegelian grand philosophy of history and the historicist particularism which keynoted the conception of the isolated historical individual.

Beginning with this orientation, Marx developed the first major bridge toward the phenomenal world, to use Kant's term. By setting Hegel on his head, he conceived of a dialectic of "material interests" which directly matched Hegel's dialectic of the *Geist* in form. This venture directly complemented the anthropological introduction of cultural pattern as a discrete elementary particle in the human field. Each intellectual movement had, in a peculiar sense, undercut the ground of the other. The anthropologists, from a naturalistic base, had come to see the "essence" of the human behavioral world in cultural-humanistic terms, whereas the Marxians, from an idealistic base, had located its essence in the interest formulated by the utilitarians. In each case, the dominant category was the one which had figured most prominently in the history of the other tradition.

Surely this was an intellectual impasse. It is in this setting that I place the movement of which the Weber-Durkheim convergence may be regarded as the core. Its most important feature was its capacity to synthesize the two great sets of intermediate categories, wants or interests on the one side and organization and relational pattern on the other side. Culture, as well as the organism and the physical world, had become inherently involved in the human behavioural sphere. This concurrently becomes the subject of an autonomous set of intellectual disciplines, neither humanities nor natural sciences. They are cultural in that they study the cultural productions of human experience, but they are at the same time analytical, oriented to empirical understanding in the sense of science.

This chapter of intellectual history has been sketchily analyzed to help make intelligible the *three*-fold structure of the intellectual disciplines in modern academic organization. It is my contention that neither the implicit empiricist-utilitarian monistic structure, in which basically all such disciplines were conceived as monolithic, nor the idealistic dualism is tenable as a frame of reference for the modern level of sophistication in this area. The social sciences must be treated as a fully autonomous category. They are not natural sciences in the sense of excluding the categories of subjective meaning, that is, they must consider knowing subjects as objects. Nor are they humanistic-cultural in the sense that the individuality of particular meanings must take complete precedence over analytical generality and such categories as causality. The emergence of sociological theorizing in the sense outlined crystallized this synthesis more sharply than any other intellectual event of recent times.

On this basis it has at last become clear that the analytical and historical components of knowledge are just that—components, not concrete classes. First, this means specifically that generalized analytical methods have become crucial, not only to economics and behaviouristic psychology, but also to the social disciplines extending much farther into the "humanistic" range, such as sociology, anthropology, law, political science, and certain aspects of history itself. Conversely, however, historical perspectives have been extended far into the normal domains of natural science. Perhaps the original crystallization of this perspective lay in "natural history's" exceedingly important role in biology. A particularly important extension of this conception went toward paleontology as the historical perspective on the whole process of organic evolution. This in turn is most intimately related to the historical aspect of geology, the "story" of the planet earth. Extension to still further ranges has become very prominent in recent times, through the historical aspect of astronomy, the history of planets, suns, and indeed galaxies.

Finally, all three sets of disciplines have their practical aspects as knowledge applied to the implementation of human values and interests, not only as fields of knowledge for its own sake. The concept of "practical reason" is not confined to any one branch of learning, but is relevant to all of them. There is, however, the essential proviso that it is exceedingly important not to confuse the two references.[22] Increasingly, this distinction seems to be becoming institutionalized in the distinction between arts and sciences faculties and the applied "professional" faculties. Equally, the underlying premises of all the intellectual disciplines require grounding at levels which are not problematic simply for the development of the individual sets of disciplines. Thus the philosophy of science is not itself a science in the sense of physics or chemistry. All the members of the triad of intellectual disciplines look both downward to the fields applying their "pure" patterns of knowledge and upward to the grounding of their premises in the more ultimate problems of the meaning of the human condition. No basic distinction can be drawn among them on either of these two accounts.

NOTES

1. There are, however, some difficult borderline problems, such as the status of law as an intellectual discipline.
2. This is extremely clear, for instance, in Hobbes's deliberate construction of his social science on the model of "geometry." See the opening chapters of Thomas Hobbes, *Leviathan*, Blackwell, Oxford, 1946.
3. On this aspect of Freud, see my article, "Social Structure and the Development of Personality," reprinted as Chapter 4 of my volume. *Social Structure and Personality*. Free Press, 1964.
4. Emile Durkheim and Marcel Mauss, *Primitive Classification*. The University of Chicago Press, 1963; French edition, 1903.
5. Just to give examples, cf. "Of Superstition and Enthusiasm," which is a kind of charter for the sociology of religion and the essays on commerce, money, trade, public credit, interest, and taxes, which are landmarks in economics. David Hume, *Essays and Treatises*, Vol. I, Cadell, London, 1793.
6. Halevy, *The Growth of Philosophical Radicalism*, Beacon Paperbacks, 1960.

7. James Olds, *The Growth and Structure of Motives.* The Free Press, 1954.
8. Talcot Parsons, *The Structure of Social Action.* McGraw-Hill, New York, 1937.
9. Wilhelm Dilthey, *Einleitung in die Geisteswissenschaften* (Duncker und Humblat, Leipzig, 1883).
10. Heinrich Rickert, *Uber die Grenzen der Naturwissenschaftichen Begriffsbildung*, 5th edition, J.C.B. Mohr. Tubingen, 1929.
11. Michel Crozier, *The Bureaucratic Phenomenon*, University of Chicago Press, 1964.
12. In these respects, Marx was more Hobbesian and Malthusian than Lockean in stressing the potentials for disrder and conflict.
13. A.N. Whitehead, *Science and the Modern World.* Macmillan Company, 1925.
14. W.B. Cannon. *The Wisdom of the Body.* A comparable view with reference to genetics is stated by H.S. Jennings, *The Biological Basis of Human Nature.*
15. See Talcott Parsons, *The Structure of Social Action*, McGraw-Hill, New York, 1937 and H. Stuart Hughes, *Consciousness and Society*, Knopf, New York, 1958 for more detailed analyses of the theoretical positions surveyed in the following Vilfredo Paraeto in sociology. Freud in psychology and the American development of social psychology, related to Pragmatism and involving James, Dewey, C.H. Cooley, G.H. Mead and W.I. Thomas.
16. Max Weber, *Max Weber on Law in Economy and Society*, Harvard University Press, 1954.
17. Max Weber, *The Religion of China*, The Free Press, Glencoe, 1951; *The Religion of India.* The Free Press, Glencoe, 1958; the original German editions of both, posthumous.
18. Here it should be noted that the comprehensive survey of religious structures translated as *The Sociology of Religion*, Beacon Press, Boston, 1962 (originally published as *Religionssoziologie in Wirtschaft und Gesellschaft*, 1922), unparalleled at the time in the analytical qualities of its approach was written as a relatively independent section of a

larger work on the relationships between the economy and other aspects of social structure.

19. Max Weber, *Gesammelte Aufsatze zur Wissenschaftslehre*, 2nd edition. Johannes Winckelmann, editor Mohr, Tubingen, 1951. Selections from this work have been translated and edited by Edward A. Shils and Henry K. Finch. *The Methodology of the Social Sciences*, The Free Press, Glencoe, 1949.

20. Emile Durkheim, *The Division of Labor in Society*. The Free Press, Glencoe, 1949 French original, 1893.

21. *Ibid.* Book I, Chap. VII.

22. The fields of engineering technology and somatic medicine, as applications of natural science knowledge, and of economic policy and of the use of psychological testing in personnel selection, as applications of social science, are relatively obvious. Sometimes, however, humanists make a virtue of their claim that the humanities are completely free of any taint of practicality—that they are fields of the pursuit of learning solely for its own sake. This claim may be doubted on one ground in particular. This is that for a considerable period in European history a humanistic education constituted the principal basis of the common culture of the elite classes of European Society—and indeed still does to a considerable extent. We may suggest that the "use" of the humanistic disciplines in giving its principal cultural character to the elite of a great civilization was just as much a "social" application as any of engineering or medicine.

[*Note*: This article is substantially drawn from the works of Talcot Parsons]

9

Educational Aims and Cultural Postures

Contemporary cosmopolitan culture is in the throes of change and conflict. Not only are we heirs of a centrifugal, disintegrating cultural force, the analytic temperament, which has gained momentum since the Renaissance, but also we have added to this heritage the implications of heavy industrialization, mass communication, urbanization, and a success orientation. The results of this heritage were spelled out in the introduction to the first section as undue intellectual specialization and compartmentalization, social estrangement, a spiritual anxiety over values, and an explosion in knowledge. These cultural phenomena have awakened us from our cultural sleep and now we are seeking and demanding of ourselves answers about the ends of which the young in our society ought to be educated. What should be transmitted to them? It is the case that they will learn something, and if we want to exercise rational guidance and control over our society, our educational goals must be outlined in a rational manner and defended with acceptable evidence.

Unfortunately questions about the aims of education are too often answered with a list of character traits, moral obligations, and political ideals which each individual ought to internalize, while no consideration is given to the cultural context in which this list is to be lived out. The difficulty with such a procedure can be seen by recognizing that it is possible to construct a theoretically defensible group of obligations and traits which are not optional in a particular culture at a particular time. For example, the ideal of rugged individualism was a character trait highly prized in the American West in the nineteenth century. One simply had to be able to fend for oneself during those hectic and demanding years. Such a character trait could be defended by saying that each man has the inalienable rights of life, liberty, and property given to him by the Creator. If this is the case, then each person should be able to exercise absolute control over his property, life, and actions. However, since persons often disagree over rights to possessions, it seems best for them to enter into a contract with each other to guarantee the protection of everyone's rights. On the basis of this contract a government is formed to regulate interpersonal relationships and to protect the life, liberty, and property of each citizen. Though rugged individualism can be argued for in this Lockean and theoretically persuasive manner, it is not a live option in a day which a high degree of conformity is needed in order to live and to earn a living. Few men work by themselves for themselves. They work in groups, in factories, in large business, in planned suburbs, and are under the constant influence of mass media. Hence, to stop a discussion of educational goals with traits and obligations viewed apart from the context in which those traits and obligations are to be lived out is to stop too soon.

Education as cultural transmission must eventually deal with the problem of deciding on culturally realistic traits and obligations to teach its young. But it must first come to grips with the central issue in any discussion of educational goals. Given contemporary American culture and its problems, what kind of attitude toward it ought to be transmitted to the young? How this problem is handled determines what the future American way of life will be. Such an attitude is more than a theoretical viewpoint objectively taken toward the way of life in which one participates. It is one's own way of life, one's own life stance, one's own cultural posture. Once one has taken a stance toward the culture in which he lives and consequently toward himself as an integral member of society, a context is established in which moral obligations and character traits find their cultural meaning. It is also on the basis of the particular cultural posture assumed by a society that it will articulate educational goals and select from the plethora of values within it those which it intends to transmit. If the crucial question about the aims of education concerns the best cultural posture to be transmitted, then what are the major alternative? Theodore Brameld has suggested at least four cultural postures which may be taken by a society toward its way of life. They are perennialism, progressivism, reconstructionism, and essentialism. In order to understand the selections in this chapter, it is important to understand not only the central point each author is making but also the historical, intellectual background of each of the cultural postures.

When attempting to find meaning in a culture its conflict, the perennialist contends that society must return to those beliefs which were fundamental to the High Middle Ages. The problem of contemporary American culture is that ever since the thirteenth century Western culture has progressively disintegrated through a loss of orientation and a growing analytical temperament. What must be recaptured is a grasp of and a living out of metaphysical principles which are extracultural, spaceless, timeless, axiomatic, transhistorical. These ultimate principles provide an authority orientation toward man, nature, and God which contemporary Americans lack and in the light of which they should attempt to adjust their lives and institutions. In an age when men seek security and meaningfulness, the perennialist position is especially appealing. The appeal is based, however, not just on the religious overtones involved in the perennialist's position but on the strong basis it has in the history of Western culture.

The first major Western philosophical figure to contribute to the perennialist viewpoint was Plato. It was his belief that reality is a realm of necessary, immutable, and eternal forms, patterns, or ideas of which men ought to come to an understanding and in terms of which they ought to conduct their lives individually and corporately. The ideals which Plato rationally defended and understood to be ultimately real were those ideals which had permeated the life of Athens during its golden age, the middle and late fifth century a B.C. In that period the ideals were expressed in mythopoeic language but they were the ideals of justice, harmony, moderation, truth, beauty, goodness. Plato believed that men living in Greece during the mid-fourth century B.C. could find meaning if they returned to those ideals of the golden age.

Aristotle disagreeing with Plato about the nature of reality contended that reality must be understood as formed-matter. There is not a realm of absolute permanence and a realm of absolute change which God has mixed together to create the world we experience, a realm of orderly change. On the contrary, permanence and change are mingled together in every object of our experience. Furthermore, all objects including humans are constantly in the process of becoming what they can and ought to become. If one is to understand objects such as humans, then one must attempt to understand the end to which they are moving, their natural end. Aristotle believed that humans are rational animals and have as their natural purpose the actualization of their physical and rational potentialities. This entails not only developing the physical dimension of the human life but also developing the rational dimension. To develop the rational dimension, a human must exercise both his practical reason in seeking the moderate path in every moral decision and his theoretical reason in contemplating the meaning of reality, the end toward which it is moving, the unmoved mover. Aristotle contends in such works as the *Politics* that men can achieve these natural and universal ends only in society, and by society he meant the *polis* as understood in the golden age of Greece. Aristotle lived during the Alexandrian period of Greek life and experienced the continued dislocation of Greek culture under the foreign influence of Macedonian rule. If he recognized any prospects for meaning coming from the cosmopolitanism of Alexander, he never mentioned it in any of his extant works. What he does advocate, however, is a return to the ideals of an earlier period and argues for those metaphysical principles and cultural ideals in a way quite distinct from Plato.

Plato and Aristotle formulated the metaphysical aspects of the perennialist position, but it was through the Christian minds of Augustine and Aquinas that Western culture has been continually influenced by the belief that in a crisis culture what men ought to do is to return to the ideals of the past. Augustine was heavily influenced by Plato as interpreted to him through the writings of Plotinus. His Christian Platonism was developed in response to the theological and political problems of the fifth century A.D. Rome, which had been the bastion of political stability and justice for over six hundred years, and was being beseiged by its perennial enemies from the North. Many Romans blamed the Christian religion for the sack of Rome in 410 A.D. by Alaric and the Visigoths. They complained that if the city gods had not been set aside by Constantine in 322 A.D., when he declared Christianity to be the official religion of Rome, then those gods would have saved their people. In 413 A.D. Augustine began writing his famous work, *The City of God*, in an effort to answer such charges. He argued that the ideals which had made Rome great in the days of the Republic were consistent with those of the Christian faith and if Romans had held to either their own ideals or to those of the Christians, they would not be experiencing the difficulties of war with the Germanic tribes. In this work and in others he employed Platonic metaphysics to express Christian meanings and developed a world view which called for men in times of cultural crisis to return to the ideals the Christian faith had always taught.

Thomas Aquinas was deeply influenced by the new

philosophical works of Aristotle which the Arabian philosophers were making available to Western Europe in the thirteenth century A.D. Although Christendom had Aristotle's *Organon* (logical works) for a long time, it did not have his metaphysical and natural science works. Challenged by these new ideas, Aquinas began to interpret Aristotle's works and to employ Aristotelian ideas in expressing the faith of the Church.

The period of Christian theological and metaphysical synthesis of the twelfth through the fourteenth centuries was the high point in the Church's thinking through to an understanding of man, nature, and God. The Schoolmen or Scholastics who effected this formulation were led by Thomas Aquinas. He believed that God created an order which should glorify Him through seeking to become what He wanted it to become. In order to achieve this purpose, each strata in the chain of being must seek to realize its fullest potential. The end of man is to become what God created him to become, and society is the context in which this purposive activity takes place. If man is to realize his God-given purposes, then the institutions and conduct of society must be arranged to aid man's pilgrimage. When faced with conflicts in culture and a concern about the aims of education, a person espousing this position has a metaphysically, theologically, and ethically sound orientation on the basis of which he can respond responsibly and constructively. The perennialist position, as it has come down through Western culture to the twentieth century, has usually been stated in Thomistic or neo-Thomist terms such as those of Jacques Maritain. However, some contemporary educational philosophers such as Robert M. Hutchins state the perennialist position in terms closer to that of Aristotle.

The most sustained attack on perennialism and at the same time the most influential educational philosophy of the twentieth century is that of progressivism. The progressivist posture toward a culture in conflict is to remain curious, flexible, tolerant, and open-minded in an effort to effect modification in the culture. His attitude is like a scientist who through adventurous exploration within an area of investigation considers the range of alternative hypotheses and gives them opportunity to prove their merit. Society should not attempt to return to the ideals of the prescientific High Middle Ages. Not only are there strong doubts about justifying knowledge claims about necessary, immutable, eternal principles but also the scientific method when applied to understanding society and how to live within it has opened up new and dependable ways of learning and effecting desirable changes. Brameld contends that the progressivist takes the "liberal road to culture" with his confidence in the native intelligence of each person living in society. Though this cultural posture is relatively new to Western culture, it has deep roots in the Western intellectual tradition.

The earliest contribution to progressivism is found in pre-Socratic philosophy. Heraclitus, a sixth century B.C. philosopher, in an attempt to determine the nature of *physis* contended that whatever exists is changing. There is nothing stable in the universe but the law of change itself. Almost a hundred years later Protagoras worked out the epistemic implications of Heraclitus' metaphysical beliefs about reality. Truth is not fixed but is temporally and spatially relative to the perceiver. The next major contribution to progressivism came during the English Renaissance and was made by Francis Bacon. Bacon reacted strongly against the old traditional authority of Scholasticism and its deductive approach to finding new knowledge. He contended that one must go to the things themselves, the objects of public experience, and with the aid of the inductive method must seek to understand them. Before one can do this, however, one must rid oneself of idols which are hindrances to finding the truth. One must eliminate the idols or prejudices which come from the nature of the mind itself (idols of the tribe), the particular enculturation of the person (idols of the den), the culturally established meanings of words (idols of the market place), and the false theories and philosophies taught in the past (idols of the theatre). Once one has rooted out these idols and has begun to approach objects themselves with an open mind and using the inductive method, one can then begin to understand. In the political thought of John Locke, progressivism finds one of its most cherished principles. It is indebted to Locke for Locke's advocacy of political freedom from the authority of the throne or from any other absolutism and for his contribution to democracy. Immanuel Kant's contention that each individual is an end in himself and not a means only is incorporated into progressivism as one of its central tenets. Although the works of Dewey seem in direct opposition to the absolutism of Hegel, he and progressivism are indebted to Hegel for the emphasis on environmentalism and the belief that reality is changing in an orderly everadjusting manner. Charles Darwin's biological investigations and his belief in evolution from lower species to higher forms of life through natural selection heavily influenced Dewey and progressivism.

The most direct influence on progressivism was the thought of Charles Sanders Peirce and William James. Peirce through an analysis of language contends that words gain meaning from what they do, from their practical effects. Also Peirce believes that meaning is achieved in community through using words which can be translated into some kind of operation. This pragmatic position about language deeply influenced Dewey's own version of pragmatism. William James continued Peirce's emphasis on the pragmatic theory of meaning. James did not advance a creed or a particular content so much as he advanced a method. For each word and belief one ought to seek "practical cash-value." Meaning and truth are not static entities written in the heart of the universe. Rather truth happens to an idea; it is part of living; indeed, truth is made by successful living. Though progressivism is varied and deeply rooted in western intellectual history, it is a peculiarly Americn philosophy and receives its best statement in the thought of John Dewey.

One more posture toward a culture in conflict is that of reconstructionism. We ought to realize that we are in a transition period from civilization to what Kenneth Boulding calls post-civilization. If this is correct, then it must be recognized that there can be no appeal either to past social institutions for orientation or to the ideals of the High Middle Ages. On the contrary, what is needed amid the conflicts and shambles of Western civilization is a reconstruction of culture. By reconstruction is meant a radical rebuilding of the culture constructed on values hammered out using the best tools and information from the social and natural sciences. The reconstruction should take a creative rebuilding approach to the contemporary cultural conflicts.

The roots of reconstructionism are as deep as those of progressivism because the reconstructionist is a modified progressivist. While the progressivist emphasizes method almost to the exclusion of ends, the reconstructionist emphasizes the method and the ends toward which society ought to move. The reconstructionist believes that the social sciences ought to be employed in the attempt to understand the culture, what its problems are, what the society in consensus desires. He is heavily indebted to the anthropologist, the sociologist, the economist, the political scientist, and the psychologist for their varied approaches and understandings of man in society. At least, in the case of Brameld, Utopian thought has influenced the reconstructionist position. Utopian works such as Plato's *Republic*, More's *Utopia*, Bellamy's *Looking Backward* point to a reconstructed understanding of society and man's place in it. These writers contend that values, orientations, and institutions of society are not what they ought to be and consequently new values, institutions, and patterns of behavior must be found and articulated. Though the reconstructionist would accept the utopian writers' emphasis on cultural critique and on the importance of developing a new culture, he would reject the otherworldly tendency in most of these works. What must be done is to employ the projective technique of the utopian writer when he is carving out a new way of life and to ground this projection in the contours of human experience and on the techniques of the social sciences.

The final cultural posture one could take in an attempt to come to grips with a culture in conflict is essentialism. The essentialism contends that what is needed for our day are stabilizers to keep us on an even keel. These stabilizers come from the culture itself, its past and present traditions and institutions. Only the time-tested content, the orderly sequence, the inherited principles, the guided discipline essential to one's culture will give one a stable perspective from which to confront the problems of a crisis culture. The essentialist position need not be one of mere acceptance of the past in a culture. Rather, it can be a critical appraisal of the importance of continuity in society and of what must be done if meaning is to be found.

Essentialism is a cultural posture which has a long heritage in Western culture. One of the first contributors to essentialism was Plato. He believed that the fourth century Greeks ought to look into their own culture and find their institutional forms and values around which they could organize their lives and answer the problems they faced in a disintegrating culture. Of course, the central institution which Plato believed ought to be maintained and its values preserved is the *polis*. He argued that the ideals which ought to govern the *polis* are a realm of forms which are necessary, immutable. At this point one can see that Plato contributed to essentialism as well as perennialism. For him the principles which are basic to the *polis* are also the perennial ones. Indeed, from Plato through Aquinas essentialism was undergirded by a metaphysics which was indistinguishable from the perennialist position. Augustine, for example, though a perennialist in that he advocated going back to the ideals of early Rome and to the early Christian faith, believed that the ideals of the Roman people and of the Christian faith are embodied in the institutions of the

Roman state and the Christian Church. In this sense Augustine contributed to the essentialist as well as to the perennialist position.

In the nineteenth century essentialism received its strongest statement in the work of Edmund Burke. Burke's position was born not of speculative metaphysics nor of scientific studies of society. Rather, he came to his views through active participation in the affairs of the English Parliament and in reaction to the American and French Revolutions. Burke believed that men are creatures of habit and find meaning and intelligibility in stable social institutions and in traditional beliefs. Any radical changes in society would sweep away these underpinnings. The French Revolution which brought about sweeping changes in the lives of Frenchmen Burke believed to be wrong. The new institutions established in the late 1790s were not based on the traditions of the French people. The effect of such changes was to uproot the people and to leave them to the whims of passion. On the other hand, the American Revolution, which was clearly based on political traditions deeply imbedded in English life, was not a radical cutting off from social institutions and beliefs and consequently was defensible.

One of the best reasoned arguments advanced by a contemporary essentialist or conservative is that made by Michael Polanyi. Polanyi does not develop his position from the position of an active politician such as a Burke or a Christian facing radical changes in society such as Augustine. After training in the natural sciences he became interested in sociology and then in philosophy, particularly in epistemology. The work of Polanyi may be more easily understood if one recognizes that he is deeply indebted to Gestalt psychology and its work in perception. Psychologists working within a Gestalt orientation contend that perception is to be explained as arising from the observer's actively organizing his cultural experience into wholes on the basis of principles brought to the learning situation. This means that in the mind's search for knowledge its point of departure is the culture in which the person lives. However, because the mind is constantly having new experiences and because of the mind's capacaity for integrating those experiences, the mind may begin to explore beyond the authority structure of a society and create new values, new understandings. Taking his cue then from the work of Gestalt psychologists, Polanyi develops an epistemology the implication of which is a social and cultural conservatism.

Penultimately, a society whose culture is in conflict and which considers carefully the ends to which it wants to educate its young and possibly its adults must recognize that it is transmitting attitudes toward itself which have important implications for the kinds of goals it wants to achieve. Particular character traits find their meaning in the context of one's attitudes toward oneself and one's society. This attitude may be called cultural posture.

Bibliography

Arendt, Hanna, *The Human Condition*, Garden City, New York: Doubleday & Company, Inc., 1959.

Bell, Daniel, *The Reforming of General Education*, New York: Columbia University Press, 1966, Chapter 4.

Berelson, Bernard, and Gary A. Stenier, *Human Behavior: An Inventory of Scientific Findings*, New York: Harcourt, Brace & World, Inc., 1964.

Boulding, Kenneth E. *The Meaning of the Twentieth Century*, New York: Harper & Row, Publishers, 1964.

Cox, Harvey. *The Secular City*, New York: Cromwell-Collier and Macmillan, Inc., 1965.

Dewey, John. *Freedom and Culture*, New York: Capricorn Books, 1963.

Dickinson, G. Lowes, *The Greek View of Life*, Second Edition. London: Methuen and Co., 1898.

Fromm, Erich, *Escape from Freedom*, New York: Avon Books, 1965.

Ginzberg, Eli (ed.) *Technology and Social Change*, New York: Columbia University Press, 1964.

Gomperz, Theodore, *Greek Thinkers*, 4 vols. New York: Charles Scribner's Sons, 1912.

Graham. Saxon. *American Culture*, New York: Harper & Row, Publishers, 1957.

Grote, G., *History of Greece*, Vols. 8 and 9.

Harris, Raymond P. *American Education*, New York: Random House, 1961.

Heilbroner, Robert L. *The Limits of American Capitalism.* New York: Harper & Row, Publishers, 1966.

Herodotus, *Histories.*

Jebb, R.C., *The Attic Orators from Antiphon to Isaeos,* 2 vols. London: Macmillan and Co., 1876.

Livingstone, R.W., *The Greek Genius and Its Meaning to Us,* Second Edition. Oxford: Clarendon Press, 1915.

May, Rollo, *Psychology and the Human Dilemma.* Princeton, New Jersey: D. Van Nostrand Company, Inc., 1967. Chapters 1, 2, 3.

Monroe, Paul, *Source Book of the History of Education, Greek and Roman Period.* New York: The Macmillan Co., 1902.

Moore, Wilbert E., *Social Change.* Englewood Cliffs, New Jersey: Prentice-Hall Inc., 1963.

Nishimoto, M., Modernization of Education and Educational Broadcasting, Tokyo, NHK Publications Associations, 1966, (in Japanese).

Pierce, John R., "Communications Technology and the Future." *Daedalus,* Vol. 94, No. 2 (Spring 1965), 506-517.

Plato, *Crito, Apology, Meno.*

Sandys, John Edwin, *A History of Classical Scholarship,* Vol. I, Second Edition, Cambridge University Press, 1906.

The Encyclopaedia Britannica, Articles: "Sophists," "Socrates," "Isocrates."

Xenophon, *Memorabilia.*

_______, *Cyropaedius.*

_______, *Oeconomicus.*

Index

A

Adam Smith, 183
Adams, Henry B., 18
Age of Pericles, 18, 29
  art and literature in, 21
Agnosticism, 32
Air Force, 8
Alfonso II, 97
Anglo-American tradition, 183
Aquinas, Thomas, 214, 219
Aristotle, 57, 147, 213, 215
Artificial jobs, 131
Asia Minor, 18, 25
Athenian gymnastics, 36
Athens, 18, 19, 20, 22, 23, 35
Attica, 19
Autolycus, 36

B

Bacon, Francis, 216
Barbarian raids, 83
Baronius, 85
Battle of Covadonga, 97
Battle of Las, 97
Beauty of speech, 43
Behaviorism, 183
Bellamy, 218
Benedict, Ruth, 191
Bernard, St., 93
Bible, 133
Boulding, Kenneth, 218
Brougham, Lord, 82
Brubacher (Prof.), 144
Burke, Edmuna, 220

C

Challis, J., 3
Charlemagne, 82, 83, 84, 85
Chivalry,
  christianizing the, 91
Choice of Hercules, 45
Christian spirit, 89
Church involved in, 84
Clergy and monks, 90
Cluny, 87, 88, 89, 93
Coleman, James, 6
Cooperation, 129
Critias, 33, 63
Cybernetics, 5

D

Darius, 31
Dark Ages', 82
  darkest part of, 86

Darwin, Charles, 164, 165, 172, 217
Darwinian biology, 203
Davenport, 176
Descartes, 181
Dewey, 130
Diagoras, 33
Dilthey, Wilhelm, 188
Drosophila, 169, 171
Durkheim, 182, 203

E

Education,
 and function of the school, 123-137
 and intellectual and moral revolution, 18-81
 and knowledge explosion, 1-17
 at the crossroads, 138-163
 concerning the aims of, 146-147
 during ninth to twelfth centuries, 82-105
 of man, 138
 paradoxes of, 157
 pride and prejudice in, 106-122
Educational aims,
 and cultural postures, 210-221
Educational and extra spheres, 158
Educational system, 159
Educational theory,
 beginning of, 68
Eliot, Charles (Prof.), 180
Emerson, 82, 106
Empedocles, 28
English Board of Education, 121
Essentialism, 219
Euripides, 33
Europe, 96
European History, 125
Euthydemus, 66, 67

F

Feudalism,
 early anarchic, 83
Fisher, R.A., 166
Freud, 181
Frogs, 36
Future-oriented society, 11

G

Games against nature, 7
German idealism, 185
Gomperz, 23, 43, 57, 59
Gorgias, 47
Grammar, 50
Greek civilization, 73, 78
Greek religion,
 traditional, 30, 33
Grundschule, 119

H

Harrison, J.W.H., 174, 175
Hebrew sages, 25
Hegel, 185
Hellenic, 77
Heredity,
 and education, 164-176
Herodotus, 27, 31
Hippias, 46-47
Human personality, 144

Huns, 85

Hutchins, Robert, M., 215

I

Information theory, 5

Inheritance,
  Mendelian theory of, 165

I.Q., 15, 113

Intellectual discipline, modern,
  philosophical background, 180
  two principal conceptions of, 182
  unity and diversity in, 177-209

Intellectual technology, 4

Intellectualism, 153

Internal freedom,
  conquest of, 147

Isocrates, 74-78

J

James, William, 217

Jebb (Prof.), 23, 71

Johnson, Samuel, 1

Judeo-Greco-Christian philosophy, 143

Justice, 61

Juvenal, 41

K

Kant, 185, 187

Kilpatrick, 130

Knowledge,
  and intelligence, 29
  discovery of universal elements in, 57
  exponential growth of, 1
  identification of, 58

L

Learning,
  advancement of and sophists, 43
  strange history of,

Livingstone, 27

Locke, 183, 217

Lucian, 30

M

Man,
  Christian idea of, 143
  scientific and philosophical-religious idea of, 141

Mapes, Walter, 93

Marathan, 19

Maritain, Jacques, 138

Marx, Karl, 191, 192, 193

Mathematics, 28

McMillan, Margret, 137

Meitner, Lise, 3

Memorabilia, 65

Michael III, 83

Mill, James, 183

Morals, study of, 61

Morgan, T.H., 170

Morgenstern, Oskar, 7

N

National Register of Scientific and Technical Personnel, 4

Nazi training, 156

New education,
  needs, 42
  opportunity, 43
  problems, 69

New social conditions, 21

Newmann, Von, 7
Novick, David, 10

O

'Old Athens',
weakness of training in, 77
Old education,
breakedown of, 35
weakness of, 35
Old morality,
breakdown of, 29
On Correct Speech, 45
Oratory,
rise of, 22
Organic Inheritance of Man,
176
Organised Complexity, 8

P

Parents' Associations, 128
Patterns of Culture, 191
Paul, 60
Periclean Revolution, 68
Pericles, 70
Persian War, 19, 34, 36, 38
Person,
social potentialities of, 150
Personality,
and individuality, 145
Philosophical thought,
beginnings of, 24
Pindar, 22, 31, 138
Plato, 37, 39, 58, 61, 69, 110,
213
Polanyi, Michael, 220
Political and economic changes,
19
Politics, 213
Post-industrial society, 15
Pragmatism, 148
Price, Derek, 1
Prodicus, 45-
Product Corporation, 16
Protagoras, 39, 44-45
Pythagoras, 28

R

Rabi, I.I., 3
Republic, 61, 110
Research and development, 10
Revolutionary underground,
183
Rhetoric, 24
and oratory, 50
Robinson, J. Harvey, 109
Roentgen, 3
Roman concept of organisation,
88

S

Saracens, 94, 96
Schwartz, Melvin, 11
Secondary School, 116
Serfs, 92
Simulation, 6
Sociologism, 151
Socrates, 37, 37, 53
disciples of, 55
doctrines of, 55
life and vocation, 54
methods of, 64
personality, 53
significance of condemnation
of, 62
view of on curriculum, 56
Sophists, 43, 44, 49, 60

Sophocles, 33
Stammler's Rudolf, 197
State,
doctrine of, 72
Synthesis,
movements towards, 189
Systems engineer, 8

T

Thales of Miletus, 25, 26, 32
The City of God, 214
The Constitution of Athens, 37
The Disciples of Isocrates, 75
Thebans, 22
Transactions of Royal Society of London, 2
Truce of God, 90

V

Verstehen, 201
Voltaire, 106
Voluntarism, 155

W

Wald, Abraham, 7
Wallace, William, 108
Wallas, Graham, 109
Weapons systems, 8
Weaver, Warren, 5
Weber, Max, 188, 196, 197, 199, 200, 203
and Emile Durkheim, 196
Wiener, Norbert, 8
Women,
education of, 73

X

Xenophanes, 28, 33
Xenophon, 56, 72-74

□□□